T0325144

"In a world where the integration of AI is advancing rapidly, *AI for Peace* provides a timely and insightful exploration of the untapped potential of AI for promoting peace, countering hate speech, protecting human rights, and addressing climate change. Paige and Branka underscore the imperative of developing AI responsibly, highlighting the ethical considerations and challenges that must accompany this challenging, interdisciplinary, but fascinating journey. As AI evolves, so must our awareness and commitment to harnessing it for the greater good. This book serves as a compelling call to action for individuals, data scientists, policymakers, and communities alike to embrace AI's positive role in creating a more peaceful world. I urge all readers to delve into its pages and reflect on the profound implications AI holds for the future of peace."

Dr. Eduard Fosch-Villaronga, *Ph.D. LL.M M.A. Associate Professor and Director of Research at the eLaw Center for Law and Digital Technologies at Leiden University (NL)*

"*AI for Peace* provides a nuanced exploration of the intricate relationship between artificial intelligence and global peace, making a compelling case for the responsible use of AI in conflict prediction, human rights, and climate action. Its rigorous analysis not only identifies the pitfalls and ethical considerations but also offers a roadmap for leveraging AI as a tool for sustaining peace and promoting social good."

Dr. Roman V. Yampolskiy, *Department of Computer Science and Engineering at the University of Louisville*

"Artificial intelligence is transforming every aspect of our politics, economics, and social affairs. Much like nuclear technologies during the post-Second World War era, AI emergence has the potential to generate monumental benefits and catastrophic harms. Predictably, concerns are growing over the misuse and weaponization of generative and general AI – from the spread of disinformation and deepfakes to the deployment of drone swarms and chimeric viruses. Yet considerably less attention is devoted to the burgeoning field of "peace tech" and the ways in which machine learning, natural language processing, and spatial processing can prevent armed conflict and build more resilient societies. Paige Arthur and Branka Panic's timely, compact, and highly readable volume – *AI for Peace* – fills this knowledge gap. Arthur and Branka have produced a fascinating overview that expertly navigates the intersections of data science, technology and peacebuilding.

"At the center of *AI for Peace* is an appeal for ethical AI governance. AI frameworks should ensure that technologies are designed and deployed to maximize fairness, inclusivity, transparency, security, privacy, accountability, as well as "peacefulness." The authors also recommend that humanitarian, development, and peacebuilding organizations adopt an "ethics in crisis" approach that enables rapid and responsible AI deployment to mitigate harms and save lives. *AI for Peace* not only builds the theoretical scaffolding for an innovative new discipline, it also offers a powerful roadmap to guide peacebuilding practice on the front lines. Arthur and Panic show that while AI can amplify hate speech, subvert privacy, and fight wars, it can also improve conflict forecasting, monitor ceasefires, counter disinformation, and wage peace."

Robert Muggah, Founder of SecDev Group and Igarapé Institute

"The authors of this book wrote their introduction in the summer of 2023, and examples from the Russo–Ukraine war are found throughout the book. By the time I am writing this review in autumn 2023, the Israel–Palestinian conflict has once again flared into open warfare with the Hamas atrocities leading to massive Israeli retaliation. Of course, as is often the case, the origins of both conflicts are far deeper: in Israel including partition in 1947, the Holocaust, early 20th century Zionism and post-Roman diaspora; and in Ukraine memories of Stalinism, second-World War Nazi-nationalist alliances, and Russification in the 18th century. When wounds can take generations to heal, is there any hope for peace?

"As a mathematician by training, I was struck by the authors' analogy of predicting conflict and predicting cloud formation. Both are positive-feedback situations where each small action may result in ever-larger consequences, the 'butterfly-wing' effect, which inevitable leads to extremes and ultimately chaos. Most often, engineers do not try to predict or manage chaos, but instead to avoid it. It is thus encouraging that this book is focused on 'peace' not as mere absence of violence, but as a positive state to seek.

"The chapters on hate speech, human rights and climate get to the heart of some of the key factors that drive violent conflict. Indeed, it has been argued that the long civil war in Syria was triggered by a combination of deep religious and ethnic divisions, human-rights abuses and the 2006–2010 drought. Similarly, behind the current Ukrainian conflict lay years of accumulating distrust between eastern and western leaning factions, and also in part a water war as the impact of the cutting off of Crimea's principal water supply in 2014 was intensified by climate-change exacerbated drought in 2020.

"At its worst, AI can intensify the cycles of mutual antagonism, accelerating the chaotic descent into violence. However, this book paints an alternative, where AI can be a force to de-escalate the language of division, to help those promoting fair societies, to bring information that can help us deal with environmental conflicts, and ultimately, as we are invited to consider in the final chapter, to ensure that a fundamental ethical principle of all AI is 'sustaining peace'."

Alan Dix, *Professorial Cardiff Metropolitan University and Director of the Computational Foundry, Swansea University Wales, UK*

AI FOR PEACE

The role of artificial intelligence in war is widely recognized, but is there also a role for AI in fostering peace and preventing conflict? *AI for Peace* provides a new perspective on AI as a potential force for good in conflict-affected countries through its uses for early warning, combating hate speech, human rights investigations, and analyzing the effects of climate change on conflict.

This book acts as an essential primer for introducing people working on peacebuilding and conflict prevention to the latest advancements in emerging AI technologies and will act as guide for ethical future practice. This book also aims to inspire data scientists to engage in the peacebuilding and prevention fields and to better understand the challenges of applying data science in conflict and fragile settings.

AI FOR EVERYTHING

Artificial intelligence (AI) is all around us. From driverless cars to game winning computers to fraud protection, AI is already involved in many aspects of life, and its impact will only continue to grow in future. Many of the world's most valuable companies are investing heavily in AI research and development, and not a day goes by without news of cutting-edge breakthroughs in AI and robotics.

The AI for Everything series explores the role of AI in contemporary life, from cars and aircraft to medicine, education, fashion and beyond. Concise and accessible, each book is written by an expert in the field and will bring the study and reality of AI to a broad readership including interested professionals, students, researchers, and lay readers.

AI for Games
Ian Millington

AI for Sports
Chris Brady, Karl Tuyls,
Shayegan Omidshafiei

AI for Learning
Carmel Kent & Benedict
du Boulay

**AI for the Sustainable
Development Goals**
Henrik Skaug Sætra

AI for School Teachers
Rose Luckin. Karine George
& Mutlu Cukurova

AI for Healthcare Robotics
Eduard Fosch-Villaronga & Hadassah
Drukarch

AI for Physics
Volker Knecht

AI for Diversity
Roger A. Søraa

AI for Finance
Edward P. K. Tsang

AI for Scientific Discovery
Janna Hastings

AI for Peace
Branka Panic & Paige Arthur

For more information about this series please visit:
https://www.routledge.com/AI-for-Everything/book-series/AIFE

AI FOR PEACE

BRANKA PANIC AND PAIGE ARTHUR

CRC Press
Taylor & Francis Group
Boca Raton London New York

CRC Press is an imprint of the
Taylor & Francis Group, an **informa** business

First edition published 2024
by CRC Press
2385 NW Executive Center Drive, Suite 320, Boca Raton FL 33431

and by CRC Press
4 Park Square, Milton Park, Abingdon, Oxon, OX14 4RN

CRC Press is an imprint of Taylor & Francis Group, LLC

© 2024 Branka Panic and Paige Arthur

Library of Congress Cataloging-in-Publication Data
Names: Panic, Branka, author. | Arthur, Paige, author.
Title: AI for peace / Branka Panic and Paige Arthur.
Other titles: Artificial intelligence for peace
Description: First edition. | Boca Raton, FL : CRC Press, 2024. |
Series: AI for everything | Includes bibliographical references.
Identifiers: LCCN 2023049593 (print) | LCCN 2023049594 (ebook) |
ISBN 9781032418384 (hardback) | ISBN 9781032418377 (paperback) |
ISBN 9781003359982 (ebook)
Subjects: LCSH: Technology and international relations. | Artificial intelligence--
Political aspects. | Artificial intelligence--Moral and ethical aspects.
Classification: LCC JZ1254 .P36 2024 (print) | LCC JZ1254 (ebook) |
DDC 327.1/72028563--dc23/eng/20231228
LC record available at https://lccn.loc.gov/2023049593
LC ebook record available at https://lccn.loc.gov/2023049594

ISBN: 978-1-032-41838-4 (hbk)
ISBN: 978-1-032-41837-7 (pbk)
ISBN: 978-1-003-35998-2 (ebk)

DOI: 10.1201/9781003359982

Typeset in Joanna
by KnowledgeWorks Global Ltd.

CONTENTS

ACKNOWLEDGMENTS

This book is the fruit of years of collaboration with a global network of technologists, researchers, and peacebuilding practitioners. While a book this short cannot do justice to the rich and varied work going on in the field, we hope it gives a glimpse into the many things that we were fortunate to learn through our combined initiatives—AI for Peace (led by Branka Panic) and the Data for Peacebuilding and Prevention program at the NYU Center on International Cooperation (led by Paige Arthur).

We feel deeply indebted to everyone we have collaborated with over the years. In a true accounting, we would list the thousands of people and organizations who have participated in our networks and events and who are themselves pushing this new field forward every day. We would like, however, to acknowledge the individuals who provided direct support as we were writing this book, whether through interviews, reviewing chapter sections, or providing general feedback. While we alone are responsible for the contents, we thank the following for their advice: Catherine Admay, Ziad Al Achkar, Aishatu Gwadabe, Håvard Hegre, Eli Mohamad, Miranda Sissons, Joshua Storck, and Martin Waehlisch.

Branka Panic, Mexico City
Paige Arthur, New York City

ABOUT THE AUTHORS

Branka Panic is the Founding Director of AI for Peace, a think tank ensuring that AI benefits peace, security, and sustainable development. Panic is a Fellow at the NYU Center on International Cooperation, Stimson-Microsoft Responsible AI Fellow, a member of UNESCO Women4Ethical AI, and a member of IEEE Global Initiative on Ethics of Autonomous and Intelligent Systems. Panic is Senior Adviser on AI and Innovation to the German Federal Foreign Office and works as Professor of Practice at the University of North Carolina. She holds an MA in International Development Policy from Duke University, Sanford School of Public Policy, and an MS in International Security from the University of Belgrade, Serbia.

Dr Paige Arthur is the Director of Global Programming at Columbia Global (Columbia University in the City of New York). Arthur was formerly Senior Fellow and Deputy Director of the NYU Center on International Cooperation, where she led the Center's work on conflict prevention and peacebuilding, including a three-year initiative on data-driven approaches to prevention. She is the author and editor of several books on transitional justice (University of Cambridge Press) and decolonization (Verso Books), and she holds a PhD from the University of California, Berkeley.

INTRODUCTION

In 2020, with the introduction of OpenAI's GPT-3, a highly advanced language generator, researchers asked the tool to write an essay to convince humans that robots are coming in peace. "Stephen Hawking has warned that AI could 'spell the end of the human race.' I am here to convince you not to worry. AI will not destroy humans. Believe me," claimed GPT-3, followed by more arguments that AI is not a threat to humanity.[1]

Fast forward a few years, and the conversation surrounding AI's peaceful nature has gained renewed prominence, coinciding with the release of ChatGPT and GPT-4. As AI becomes increasingly integrated into autonomous society, concerns arise regarding the possibility of catastrophic events that could stem from its implementation.

In response to these concerns, in 2023, a letter was released from industry leaders, researchers, and other observers, urging for a pause on research on all AI systems surpassing the capabilities of GPT-4, which they refer to as "giant AI experiments."[2] While examining the potential threats posed by generative and general AI is crucial, it is equally important to acknowledge the possible negative impacts and potential misuse of narrow AI. From the deployment of drone swarms armed with advanced weaponry that could serve as sophisticated weapons of mass destruction to the exploitation of facial recognition for surveillance and human rights abuse, as well as the creation of AI-generated deepfakes (fraudulent videos, images, and text), the risks associated with AI technology are multifaceted and demand further attention. Indeed, AI is a growing element in the military strategy of many countries, and investments in defense and national security are rising every year. Military uses

DOI: 10.1201/9781003359982-1

of AI are multiple and advanced, in warfare, situational awareness and threat monitoring, autonomous weapons systems, and battle-field healthcare.

A BURGEONING FIELD OF "PEACE TECH"

By contrast, exploring and utilizing "AI for peace" has been limited, even though this is a growing field of work that also intersects with many other fields. We describe how citizens, data scientists, policy-makers, and communities can be empowered to use AI to build and sustain peace in their countries.

But what is peace? In this book, we follow the consensus of peace-building practitioners that peace should be understood not as a nega-tive term—the absence of violence—but rather as a positive one—the presence of social trust, resilience to violence, and strong civic and community institutions to manage conflicts when they (inevitably) arise. Peace is a holistic concept that draws on many different facets of human relationships, from economic security to social trust to socio-emotional wellbeing, among others. In this book, we do not have space to cover every topic relating to peaceful societies; rather, we survey some of the most important developments for people working in this field and those hoping to contribute to it.

The use of AI for peace is new, and it has been driven by the revo-lutions in data and technologies that have taken place over the last few years. These revolutions have generated volumes of data (satellite, video, images, news, text, etc.) that are growing at a massive speed, scale, and frequency. They also resulted in highly advanced sta-tistical modeling and the use of AI, including machine learning, neu-ral networks, and natural language processing, to analyze that data. One example of how quickly change is happening is the advance from GPT-3.5 (ChatGPT) to GPT-4, which took less than 6 months.

Peacebuilders have already been using new technologies—not necessarily AI-driven—to do a variety of things. There is much about the digital and data revolution that has had positive benefits for peace work. There has been an explosion of useful data to help understand how strong societies are, where their institutions to regulate conflict may be weak, and to help guide decisions about how to strengthen them further. Peacebuilders have also seized upon a myriad of practical applications. They have used human review of satellite images to detect evidence of war crimes in Darfur; they have used mobile cell phone networks to warn communities of potential militia attacks in remote areas of the Democratic Republic of the Congo; and they have used social media platforms to share ideas, connect with one another, organize against authoritarian governments, publicize human rights abuse, and generate social movements for justice.[3] In their daily work, peacebuilders have drawn upon productivity tools like automated translation (and now ChatGPT) to improve their ability to communicate efficiently and effectively.

These applications are relevant both to countries that are currently peaceful (to help them stay that way) and to those that are emerging from violent conflict. Indeed, AI may contribute even to sensitive peace negotiation processes between warring parties. People involved in peace processes can already take advantage of digital tools like satellite images and geographic information systems (GIS) to monitor ceasefires and the disengagement of military forces. During peace negotiations themselves, which have usually been the domain of a small elite, negotiators and mediators can also draw on AI-driven tools to ensure that the peace process taps into the broader public sentiment around key conflict issues—which may not be fully represented by the elite men (most often) sitting at the table. For example, the United Nations has developed a tool for sentiment analysis and opinion mining using natural language processing of public social media sources. AI can help mediators see patterns, anticipate stumbling blocks in the negotiation, and make sure that there is a broader buy-in to the key terms of the agreement than that of only the conflict leaders. All of this will contribute to a greater likelihood that a peace agreement, once signed, will actually endure.

In short, AI-driven tools are just one part of a larger set of human and machine "technologies" that peacebuilders can draw upon in their work, depending on their needs and the ethics of using them.

GOALS AND PLAN OF THE BOOK

Our aim is to provide a fresh perspective on AI as a potential force for good for peace and in already conflict-affected regions. We delve into the diverse technologies in the AI landscape, such as machine learning, natural language processing, and image processing—and demonstrate how, when ethically used, these can be harnessed to collect and process vast amounts of data, uncover patterns, and enhance the work of peacebuilders. We also shed light on risks and emphasize the importance of embedding ethics in all stages of AI-enabled activities—design, development, and implementation. It is imperative that those dedicated to peace navigate this landscape with caution, balancing the potential benefits of AI with an awareness of its malicious use and unintended consequences.

This book is an introduction to the latest advancements in emerging technologies and encourages practitioners, especially, to take a more active role in the use of AI in their work. At the same time, the book speaks to data scientists and AI experts, raising their awareness about the impacts of their work beyond bias and transparency and adding a peace and prevention lens to their work. It will also empower them to bring their technical expertise to the peacebuilding field.

We cannot hope to be comprehensive in addressing two such large and multifaceted fields: AI and peace. There are sadly a number of fascinating issues we have not had space to cover, such as how "smart cities" (which deploy sensors in urban areas to collect useful data for managing urban spaces) could be designed with the aims of peacebuilding, conflict prevention, and social cohesion in mind, or how AI-driven tools are starting to be used by UN peacekeepers in some of the world's most challenging contexts.

Our chapters therefore capture key aspects of innovation— and hopefully make readers curious enough to start asking further questions. Beyond describing AI innovations, we take care in each chapter to explain what the specific challenges are for peace for each topic, because this broader understanding helps to explain why AI tools can be relevant to solving those challenges.

In Chapter 1, we start with conflict prediction. This is because preventing violent conflict *before* it starts is the goal of every person in this field, given the devastation of war. We describe how risk for conflict is assessed, as well as the important AI-assisted gains that have been made in the past ten years in forecasting which countries are at highest risk for violence. But we also show both the limits of current modeling and why predicting conflict onset—when a peaceful society will tip into war—is such a hard problem. We look at new approaches, such as AI-assisted efforts to better understand why countries are peaceful, rather than why they fall into conflict.

In Chapter 2, we look at hate speech because this is a key method by which leaders create polarization and mobilize populations for violence. Our focus is on how AI has not only led to the massive proliferation of hate speech but is also being used to detect, limit, and actively counter it. Understanding how to fight hate speech is also important, given the parallels with the political uses of misinformation and disinformation. When citizens' arguments (and deep beliefs) are based on misinformation, deep fakes, and hateful stereotypes, the risk of tipping into violence can be greater. While much of this chapter focuses on content that is proliferating on the big social media platforms, we also give some examples of other groups that are using AI to detect and counter hate speech.

In Chapter 3, we survey the positive uses of AI to support human rights, especially in conflict-affected countries. Respect for human rights is essential to peace, and the erosion of rights is a warning signal that a society may be tipping into violence. We condemn the many violations of rights for which AI-enabled surveillance technologies are being used, but our focus here is on the citizens, activists, and scientists who are bending this technology for their own peaceful and rights-protecting ends. We conclude the chapter by showing how human rights frameworks are useful for curbing some of the most pernicious social effects of AI-enabled technologies.

Chapter 4 tackles an area of growing urgency: climate change. We raise awareness of the promise and perils of AI for understanding the relationship between conflict and climate change, and we explore new tools for anticipating, preventing, and responding to climate-related conflict. Our aim is to explore the potential for building planet-centered technologies as well as foster more informed climate- and conflict-aware technologists, data scientists, designers, engineers, and technology activists.

As we navigate the intricate intersection of AI and peace, we remain mindful of the ethical considerations and challenges that accompany this rapidly evolving landscape. In Chapter 5, the concluding chapter of this book, we grapple with the ethical dilemmas surrounding the "AI for peace" concept, examining the risks associated with biases, privacy infringements, unintended consequences, digital colonialism, and the pressing imperative for responsible and accountable design, development, and implementation.

This book aims to raise awareness and serve as a call for action for humanity to seize the momentum in rights-respecting, ethical AI development—and steer it towards a future in which AI aids humanity in sustaining peace, rather than perpetuating wars.

CONCLUSION

While this book illustrates the potential for AI to contribute to sustaining peace, the prevention of violent conflict, and the safeguarding of human rights, it is vital to acknowledge that AI alone is not a panacea.

Ultimately, while AI can be a valuable tool to address various challenges of conflict and peace (when used responsibly), achieving peace requires multifaceted approaches that encompass not only technological innovation but also human peacebuilders who understand peacemaking and conflict resolution practices, how to foster social and economic development, and the practice and politics of coordinating the collective efforts of governments, international organizations, and citizens themselves.

As we write this introduction in summer of 2023, we are keenly aware that this book may go quickly out of date. Our hope is that this work—which is a narrow snapshot in time—will provide a common point of departure for future innovation and collaboration among peacebuilders, technologists, policymakers, and others. By harnessing the capabilities of ethical AI to advance peacebuilding efforts, we can strive towards a future where technology and humanity converge to foster lasting peace.

NOTES

1 "A Robot Wrote This Entire Article. Are You Scared Yet, Human?," *The Guardian*, September 8, 2020, https://www.theguardian.com/commentisfree/2020/sep/08/robot-wrote-this-article-gpt-3?fbclid=IwAR2AJgp1HdtYao-XYYGv23J48Sup1ZJKEeT566azx1cr2mkUhdp5x7Obb6w.

2 Cade Metz and Gregory Schmidt, "Elon Musk and Others Call for a Pause on A.I., Citing 'Profound Risks' to Society," *The New York Times*, March 29, 2023, https://www.nytimes.com/2023/03/29/technology/ai-artificial-intelligence-musk-risks.html.

3 Branka Panic, "Peacebuilding and Prevention Ecosystem Mapping: The State of Play and the Path to Creating a Community of Practice," Center on International Cooperation, 2020, October 27, 2020, https://cic.nyu.edu/resources/data-for-peacebuilding-and-prevention-ecosystem-mapping-the-state-of-play-and-the-path-to-creating-a-community-of-practice/.

1

AI AND CONFLICT PREDICTION

OUR REACH EXCEEDING OUR GRASP

Since at least Nostradamus in the sixteenth century, the possibility of predicting the onset of war has ignited the imagination in the hope that people could therefore prevent it. Books, television, and movies have unleashed multiple visions of a super-human AI so powerful that it could predict patterns of human behavior accurately—and that they could then eliminate threats to peace. The idea of "AI for peace" includes dark examples, like Ultron in the twenty-first century Marvel movies, in which a "peacekeeping" AI turns on humanity, and the AI in the television series Westworld, which predicts the behavior of individual humans in order to eliminate violence—but ends up being used for violent and coercive ends. But the idea also includes more positive ones, such as the mid-twentieth-century invention of Hari Seldon's "psychohistory" in Isaac Asimov's Foundation novels, in which prediction aims to guide humanity toward a more peaceful future.

Yet our imagination has outpaced our capabilities. The reasons for peace breaking down and violent conflict breaking out are complex and contingent on highly local factors, including the discussions and decisions of individual leaders—much of which may be deliberately secretive. There is no AI on the horizon that could

DOI: 10.1201/9781003359982-2

turn these fictions into reality. Identifying in advance the specific moment when a foreign leader has decided to invade (as Putin did in Ukraine in February 2022) or when a society's institutions are so weak that it will tip from an uneasy peace into mass violence (like in Rwanda in April 1994) is not yet within our grasp.

Instead, researchers have more successfully focused on using the power of data to identify *rising risks for violence* and forecast *potential hot spots*. In other words, AI so far is most likely to help us prepare for the possibility of conflict, without knowing for sure whether it will erupt with absolute certainty. And, indeed, there is a lot of promise for AI to take this kind of modeling to the next level. In this chapter, we will: better understand violent conflict and what makes it difficult to predict; review the pioneering efforts to identify rising risks and hot spots, with a focus on how AI has enabled better and more use of data; assess the challenges to using AI in predicting conflict; and look to the future of AI in conflict prediction.

UNDERSTANDING AND PREVENTING VIOLENT CONFLICT

All societies have conflict. In more peaceful societies, conflict is managed successfully through local and national institutions, such as community boards, legislatures, courts, and (in many countries) bodies to negotiate between workers and private companies. Between countries, conflicts are managed through diplomacy and treaties, as well as through regional and global bodies, such as the United Nations.

These institutions do not always work well; they may constantly change, and they may be challenged by groups that feel excluded. Indeed, all societies have also, at one point or another in their histories, experienced *violent* conflict, whether this is civil war (such as in the United States and Spain) or interstate war, like World Wars I and II (1914–1918 and 1939–1945). Sometimes, civil wars and interstate wars go hand in hand, like in the First and Second Congo Wars (1996–1997 and 1998–2003), which included countries neighboring the Democratic Republic of Congo.

In recent years, researchers have refined arguments and evidence for the causes of violent conflict—especially violent conflict used to control, contest, or take over a state. Researchers have focused on better understanding the different roles of *greed* (economic motivations) and *grievance* (real and perceived injustice and inequality between ethnoreligious, regional, and other groups) as motives for violent conflict. They have explored what happens when political and social institutions are too weak to resolve conflicts peacefully.

In short, they have built a good body of evidence for the main *structural* factors driving violent conflict, which is critical to the effective use of AI to help with forecasting and prediction. There are many structural factors (from economic development to geography to governance, etc.), but we can understand them through a few examples.[1] Take inequality, which is mentioned above. Inequalities in wealth and political participation between groups in a society—for example, ethnic groups or regional groups—are important. Such inequalities can give rise to grievances and calls for reform, which, if not met, can lead to war or calls for secession. A second example is the existence of low levels of trust in the government, especially in countries where the government is not seen to deliver basic public goods to people, like security and simple infrastructure. As a result, people may turn to non-state groups to provide security, food, and healthcare at the local level—setting up a challenge to the government and the potential for violence. When it comes to conflict between countries, key factors include a range of real and perceived threats to security. Such threats can be military, such as the buildup of weapons or forces, but they can also be nonmilitary, such as the control of energy supplies needed by neighbors. When this happens, we typically see countries take steps to protect themselves—which can in turn be seen as a threat by the *other* country. This can trigger a dangerous escalation of mistrust.

Structural factors like inequality, low trust, and insecurity set the conditions. But on their own, they do not provide enough information to predict the specific tipping point for escalation and the onset of violent conflict. Here is where researchers have emphasized the importance of considering the dynamic *processes* by which groups and leaders in conflict mobilize, repress, and negotiate with one another. As Robert A. Blair and Nicholas Sambanis point out, "Structural characteristics tend to make poor predictors of the timing of civil war onset and often cannot distinguish between violent and nonviolent conflict. Grievances alone are not sufficient to explain the escalation of nonviolent conflicts into violent ones. ...Process-based research on conflict escalation has focused in particular on the role that state repression or accommodation of claim-making groups can play in dynamically altering the costs and benefits of rebellion."[2] Indeed, a key challenge now is to predict where conflict will erupt in previously peaceful societies. This is because there is a "conflict trap" for countries—once they have a conflict, it is much more likely to re-erupt and, therefore, easier to predict.

Thus, both structural and process-oriented factors are important for understanding conflict. Can AI help? Let us look at what has been tried so far.

PREDICTION AND FORECASTING: INITIAL ATTEMPTS

Using this body of evidence, over the past decade, social scientists in the United States, Europe, and beyond have started to tap into the potential of larger data sets and AI to take the leap from describing and explaining violent conflict to providing a forecast of where and when it might take place. Why? Because this information could be critically important to political leaders, citizens, policymakers, and others who might be able to help prevent a crisis or minimize the devastation that results from it. Conflicts can cause mass human suffering; wreak havoc on communities, economies, and environments; and break essential bonds of trust among citizens and the government. It would be better to avoid or reduce these harms than to spend decades trying to repair them. Some of these efforts have taken place in the private sector, with companies like Lockheed Martin and Palantir making efforts—not without controversy as their work is not public and has mainly been used by governments. We focus here on more openly available options, mainly from the public and academic sectors.

While the revolution in data quantity has created new opportunities for modeling, what seems immediately clear is that big data alone cannot transform the study and prediction of violent conflict. The flood of information one could potentially have access to (for example, social media posts, search engine data, cellular network data, satellite images, etc.) would seemingly put real-time information about conditions on the ground directly into the hands of social scientists. But researchers still face the same problems with the quality and relevance of the data as they would with a smaller data set—with the challenge greatly magnified given the sheer scale of the information, much of which might be mis/disinformation. In the end, social scientists still must select the data most relevant to the phenomenon being predicted, and this requires a rigorous research design and significant testing.

This is one reason that many social scientists have not primarily used big data (as yet) in order to help with the forecasting and prediction of violent conflicts. Instead, they continue to rely on more traditional, vetted data sources on organized, politically related violence and crisis, such as the Political Instability Task Force (PITF), the Armed Conflict Location and Event Data (ACLED), and the Uppsala Conflict Data Program (UCDP). They have also integrated, among others, trusted data from development agencies about economic development and data about a country's governance and political institutions—for example, the Varieties of Democracy project (V-Dem). This said, some have also tapped into larger data sets. This includes global news-related data, for example, from the AI-driven Global Database of Events, Language, and Tone (GDELT), among others.

Many of these data sets already rely on AI—specifically, natural language processing and text classification techniques—to generate data. For example, one of the main sources of data on armed conflict, ACLED, has been using machine learning to help classify types of protest events around the globe. The Carter Center, in partnership with Microsoft's AI for Good team, has also used text classification (specifically, BERT) for projects to track conflict dynamics in Syria.[3]

Mainly using a wide variety of data from smaller, trusted data sets, researchers have used machine learning techniques to achieve a measure of success in forecasting violent conflict—especially in the short term and especially in countries where there is already a degree of violent conflict, often measured in terms of the number of "battle-related" deaths. Machine learning is used for detecting patterns and finding relationships among the data, helping to determine which conflict factors are most salient in which countries.

A 2023 review of conflict and mass violence forecasting systems showed that half of such systems surveyed are already using machine learning algorithms to help identify patterns and generate forecasts. Many of these are using random forest algorithms, which operate through vast decision trees that work through large data sets to yield a result.[4] A noteworthy example of this use is the Violence & Impacts Early-Warning System (ViEWS), a consortium between the University of Uppsala and the Peace Research Institute–Oslo, which aims to forecast the potential for political violence in Africa and the Middle East. While there are many examples of how natural language processing and machine learning are being used to strengthen forecasting, ViEWS provides a good synopsis of how researchers are incorporating new techniques and addressing previous failings.[5]

The goal of ViEWS is to predict the number of fatalities in impending state-based conflict in the coming 1–36 months. It relies on more than 200 different country-level predictors, including conflict history data (UCDP, ACLED), political institutions (V-Dem), a variety of development indicators, as well as news monitoring sources.[6] In recent years, it has updated its methodology to use random forest classifier algorithms to train sub-models. It then uses a genetic algorithm to weight the sub-models in ensembling them together for the forecasting.[7] ViEWS is trying to straddle the divide between structural and process-related indicators of violence by including data on both longer term trends and indicators of rising instability, such as protests. Additionally, it aims to update its data at least once a year, but ideally once a month, as available. This update is important as violence dynamics can change very quickly.

How well do the forecasts of ViEWS and other systems hold up? For ViEWS, in most cases, the actual number of fatalities is between 50 percent and 200 percent of the predicted level. An exception, however, is when ViEWS predicts between 3 and 10 fatalities, in which case there is a sizeable share of instances where the actual fatalities exceed 20—sometimes significantly so.[8]

More generally, the 2023 review (mentioned above) of several forecasting models assesses forecasts for African countries for the year 2020. It shows, first, that the models included in the review drew similar conclusions about the countries at highest risk for conflict, including Sudan, Nigeria, and Somalia, among others. They also generally showed the potential for a higher risk of violence in countries that actually did see violence—for example, in Ethiopia, which erupted in conflict toward the end of 2020. However, most of the systems suggested a static risk over time that saw little change. What is needed from a policy perspective, however, is to show finer grained shifts that would indicate a *rapidly* escalating risk (like in Ethiopia), rather than just a general risk without a sense of whether that risk is quickly increasing or decreasing.[9]

In other words, no one has yet found a "magic bullet" for predicting conflict or crisis. And perhaps we should not expect to find this violent conflicts are complex, aggregated events, with different root causes in different places, rather than single outcomes—for some observers, predicting them is more like trying to predict the onset of a complex financial crisis than predicting a more simple, single measure like the inflation rate.[10] An interesting conclusion so far is that the drivers of instability themselves change, and so models must change as well. For example, a pioneering model that was very good at predicting country-level political instability between 1995 and 2004 (predicting 85.7 percent of events) did a much poorer job for events between 2005 and 2013 (predicting only 35.3 percent of events). Importantly, it did not predict significant Arab Spring crises in 2011 (Egypt, Syria, or Libya).[11]

Indeed, where the models have shown the greatest promise so far is in predicting changes in violence when a conflict is *already* underway—rather than predicting the start of a violent conflict in a previously peaceful society.[12] New research is currently in progress to tackle the "hard problem" of forecasting conflict onset, including a prediction competition organized by the ViEWS team.[13]

LOCALIZED DETECTION MODELS

On a remote hillside in Syria, someone taps their phone to open an app. It is 2018, and planes are making bombing runs on civilian targets. The person is part of a network of "spotters" who watch the skies for aircraft and upload sightings into the Sentry app by Hala Systems. The information is transmitted to Hala, a US-based company. Hala integrates it with their own data from remote acoustic sensors positioned in Syria, which record sounds that can help identify the type and speed of the planes. An AI-enabled program helps to determine if the plane is a threat and if a warning should go to civilians in the area through Hala's smartphone app.[14]

Social scientists' attempts to predict the onset or escalation of conflict, as described in the previous section, are not the only valuable approach. Also important is the ability to offer "early warnings" that violence may be imminent so that people can seek protection or governments can put resources in place to help. Hala Systems has been at the leading edge of using AI to put early warning signals directly into the hands of people in harm's way. But there are many other initiatives that are attempting to provide similar information. For example, when violence is imminent, people often leave their homes in mass. The UN Refugee Agency's (UNHCR) Project Jetson experiment is now using machine learning algorithms for large-scale data on issues like food insecurity and violence to predict displacement in Somalia.[15] The Danish Refugee Council has also developed a machine learning-driven prediction model for displacement from one to three years in the future, claiming that half of the predictions are accurate more than 90 percent of the time.[16] When an indicator of imminent movement is noticed, governments or the UN can put resources in place or act diplomatically to try to address the underlying causes, including conflict.

Using natural language processing, AI, remote sensing, visioning, and other AI-driven technologies has the potential to improve these existing, more localized initiatives to stop violence in its tracks or allow people to seek safety. Some of these initiatives rely heavily on local people reporting on events they observe. For example, the Economic Community of West African States has a network of human monitors across the region that regularly feed observations into a central Early Warning System based in Nigeria. And the Kivu Security Tracker in eastern Congo has a network of monitors who use text messaging and cell phones to send warnings into a central database, which can then be shared out with communities at risk. While this kind of real-time observational data can be critical to protecting people, human monitors cannot see everything, and they bring their own biases. To the extent that more and different kinds of data can complement human observers, including using AI, systems may be improved.

HOW AI CAN HELP

The dream of using AI to replace the judgment of experts and their more traditional information sources is still far off. But AI is already proving essential in a several ways.

First, researchers are benefiting from using natural language processing to convert text to usable data. Having a machine help with tasks reduces the amount of time and work that human researchers need to use. This is already being done, although it does not eliminate the need for human supervision and vetting of the data being produced.

Second, machine learning methods like random forest (as well as others that are increasingly used for conflict prediction, like neural networks) can move through large, diverse data sets more efficiently than traditional models. And they have the potential to yield new insights about the most relevant conflict factors for different countries.[17] Random forest is one of the most commonly used, as it works both for the classification of unlabeled data (unsupervised learning) and for regressions to understand relationships between dependent and independent variables (supervised learning). Both of these uses are valuable in current attempts to forecast conflict.

Third, use of AI is enabling more accurate prediction, which is in turn strengthening empirical evidence for testing theories of conflict onset and escalation. It may be surprising, but in the past, many models for conflict or crisis were evaluated based on whether their results were "statistically significant"—not the degree to which the models could actually make correct predictions. Now more and more researchers are arguing that for a theory to be valid, it should also be able to predict (not just explain). AI techniques have already proven to be essential in creating the out-of-sample data needed for testing and prediction of models on "real-world" situations that are not already included in the model.

Finally, the ensembling of different models to reduce or average out errors is already a standard feature of forecasting approaches. Researchers have used both boosting and stacking algorithms to learn how to best combine the models or to create a weighted average of predictions. Deeper use of ensembling algorithms will be a big part of the future.

CHALLENGES

Predicting conflict is difficult, especially when the conflict takes place in a previously peaceful country. There is always a degree of uncertainty involved. Some believe that conflict "onset"— that is, where it is new and not part of a conflict trap or cycle of violence—is inherently resistant to modeling. Onset relates to things that may be fundamentally hard for AI: people breaking rules rather than following them; miscommunication ("information failures") between conflict parties; and even secrecy and hiding information (and data) that would help give a fuller picture of the dynamic to outsiders. Some argue that behaviors around conflict are fundamentally different than the kinds of behaviors researchers typically try to predict, such as voting and consumption patterns.[18] In fact, there may still be some reason to think that human forecasters may do as well as machine learning models (so far) when it comes to conflict—some researchers have shown the promise of human "superforecasters" to predict more complex social phenomena.[19]

In addition, even with the models and algorithms we currently have, there are challenges around the quality, availability, and quantity of data. Accurate forecasting needs reliable data and measures for things that can be predicted. Researchers have relied on the smaller data sets mentioned above because these are trusted and reliable sources. Once you move to big data—for example, social media posts—it becomes much harder to trust the data and to filter out false information.

And you need a lot of this data—not just for right now, but for very long periods of time, including historically. The field suffers from the "curse" of small data. It is simply hard to get the required data in conflict zones or in countries that don't yet have strong statistics-gathering infrastructures. When researchers do get the data, it can be very "noisy," which makes it difficult for machines to use. Furthermore, small data sets can lead to biases in the outcomes, which requires special attention and techniques to prevent, including averaging data from multiple sources.

Finally, some are skeptical that such prediction is even possible. There is an open question about whether predicting violent conflict is like predicting the formation of clouds (so far impossible) or predicting the functioning of clocks (highly possible). Some lean toward seeing conflicts like clouds—irregular and disorderly rather than regular and orderly.[20] Even with the power of AI-related techniques, it is unclear whether we should ever expect to predict the eruption of conflict with certainty.

THE FUTURE OF AI AND CONFLICT FORECASTING

This skepticism is not going to stop people from trying to predict when societies may tip away from peace, or at least to raise the red flag when the risk of conflict appears imminent. This is because the stakes are just too high in terms of human suffering, economic collapse, and environmental degradation. AI has shown promise in improving forecasting techniques, but human expertise on conflict situations and dynamics remains essential so far.

The future of AI and conflict prediction leads in at least three directions. One direction, which is only beginning to be explored, is to use AI methods to better understand why societies are peaceful or how they come to be peaceful after a period of conflict. Machine learning analysis (specifically, random forest) has been used, for example, by researchers trying to understand the complex variables of "peace systems"—clusters of neighboring communities who do not go to war with one another.[21] This information could be used by citizens and policymakers to strengthen the resilience of their communities.

A second direction is the grand ambition that, one day, AI methods will have advanced to the degree that "brute force" analysis of ever larger, big-data sets will yield the kind of global forecasts of violent conflict that have so far eluded researchers.[22] AI evangelists are likely to see this as a possibility, even if it remains far-fetched for others.

A final direction is for future efforts to have a more limited spatial and temporal scope in predicting conflict, but with higher credibility—for example, forecasting the "projected short-term trajectories of violence in a given city in an ongoing civil war" rather than a magic bullet for conflict onset, which has inherent complexities and limitations.[23] This kind of approach would incrementally add data sources as they are ready and reliable (such as news sources, sentiment analysis, and satellite images) in order to deepen and refine prediction models. We could imagine finer grained and more accurate short-term predictions emerging, which would be actionable for policymakers, governments, and local communities. Researchers could use AI-enabled knowledge graph techniques to synthesize and pose questions to large bodies of specialized knowledge about conflict drivers and the dynamic relationships between them. This is more likely to be within our grasp.

One facet of this approach can also be to provide better predictions of the impact of conflict—and the cost of inaction when the risks of violence are high. This is important because, in both national and global debates, policymakers have long asked for improved cost–benefit analysis to justify investment in preventive actions; they are reluctant to spend money on prevention or peacebuilding if they are not sure it will be money well spent. That is, how do they know if they spend funds on certain kinds of preventive actions to strengthen peace, that this will yield a positive result and therefore "pay off" in the form of averting the massive human, economic, and environmental losses that war causes? Answering this kind of question is critical to getting governments to invest in preventing conflict and fostering peace in the first place. The ongoing advances described in this chapter could make a profound difference in starting to answer this question.

NOTES

1 For a comprehensive overview, see United Nations and World Bank, *Pathways for Peace: Inclusive Processes to Preventing Violent Conflict* (UN–World Bank Group, 2018).

2 Robert A. Blair and Nicholas Sambanis, "Forecasting Civil Wars: Theory and Structure in an Age of 'Big Data' and Machine Learning," *Journal of Conflict Resolution* 64, no. 10 (2020/11/01 2020): 1885–915.

3 Anusua Trivedi, Kate Keator, Michael Scholtens, Brandon Haigood, Rahul Dodhia, Juan Lavista Ferres, and Ria Sankar, "How to Handle Armed Conflict Data in a Real-World Scenario?" *Philosophy & Technology* 34, no. Suppl 1 (Nov. 2021): 111+.

4 Espen Geelmuyden Rød, Tim Gåsste, and Håvard Hegre, "A review and comparison of conflict early warning systems," *International Journal of Forecasting* (2023), https://doi.org/10.1016/j.ijforecast.2023.01.001.

5 The ViEWS project's homepage is at https://viewsforecasting.org.

6 ViEWS project homepage at https://viewsforecasting.org. On the use of news sources, see Hannes Mueller, and Christopher Rauh, "Reading between the Lines: Prediction of Political Violence Using Newspaper Text," *American Political Science Review* 112, no. 2 (2018): 358–75.

7 Håvard Hegre, Curtis Bell, Michael Colaresi, Mihai Croicu, Frederick Hoyles, Remco Jansen, Maxine Ria Leis, Angelica Lindqvist-McGowan, David Randahl, Espen Geelmuyden Rød, and Paola Vesco, "ViEWS2020: Revising and evaluating the ViEWS political Violence Early-Warning System," *Journal of Peace Research* 58, no. 3: 599–611. On the genetic algorithm, see The ViEWS Team, "Forecasting fatalities" (May 31, 2022), http://uu.diva-portal.org/smash/get/diva2:1667048/FULLTEXT01.pdf; accessed on June 23, 2023.

8 ViEWS, "Forecasting fatalities in armed conflict: forecasts for April 2022 to March 2025" (May 2022), http://uu.diva-portal.org/smash/get/diva2:1665945/FULLTEXT01.pdf; accessed on June 23, 2023.

9 Geelmuyden Rød, Gåsste, and Hegre, "A review and comparison of conflict early warning systems."

10 Drew Bowlsby, Erica Chenoweth, Cullen Hendrix, and Jonathan D. Moyer, "The Future Is a Moving Target: Predicting Political Instability," *British Journal of Political Science* 50, no. 4 (2020): 1405–17.

11 Ibid.

12 Hegre et al., "VIEWS2020."

13 See, e.g., Hannes Mueller, Christopher Rauh, and Alessandro Ruggieri, "Dynamic Early Warning and Action Model" (Barcelona School of Economics: BSE Working Paper 1355: 2022); and Håvard Hegre, Paola Vesco & Michael Colaresi, "Lessons from an escalation prediction competition," *International Interactions* 48, no. 4 (2022): 521–554.

14 Louisa Loveluck, "The secret app that gives Syrian civilians minutes to escape airstrikes," *The Washington Post*, August 18, 2018; https://www.washingtonpost.com/world/the-secret-app-that-gives-syrian-civilians-minutes-to-escape-airstrikes/2018/08/17/e91e66be-9cbf-11e8-b55e-5002300ef004_story.html.

15 See UNHCR's website for Project Jetson at https://jetson.unhcr.org/.

16 Danish Refugee Council, "Foresight: Displacement Forecasts," https://pro. drc.ngo/what-we-do/innovation-and-climate-action/predictive-analysis/ foresight-displacement-forecasts/; accessed May 15, 2023.

17 Hegre, Vesco, and Colaresi, "Lessons from an escalation prediction competition."

18 Lars-Erik Cederman and Nils B. Weidmann, "Conflict Prediction: Time to Adjust our Expectations?" *Science* no. 355 (2017), 2.

19 See Philip E. Tetlock, Barbara A. Mellers, and J. Peter Scoblic, "Bringing Probability Judgments into Policy Debates Via Forecasting Tournaments," *Science* 355, no. 6324 (2017): 481–83. Tetlock and Mellers have also co-founded a consultancy to provide superforecasting services: https://good-judgment.com/about/our-team/.

20 Thomas Chadefaux, "Early Warning Signals for War in the News," *Journal of Peace Research* 51, no. 1 (2014): 5–18.

21 Douglas P. Fry, Geneviève Souillac, Larry Liebovitch, Peter T. Coleman, Kane Agan, Elliot Nicholson-Cox, Dani Mason, Frank Palma Gomez, and Susie Strauss, "Societies within Peace Systems Avoid War and Build Positive Intergroup Relationships," *Humanities and Social Sciences Communications* 8, article 17 (January 18, 2021).

22 Cederman and Weidmann, "Conflict Prediction: Time to Adjust our Expectations?" 3.

23 Ibid.

2

AI AND HATE SPEECH

THE ROLE OF ALGORITHMS IN INCITING
VIOLENCE AND FIGHTING AGAINST IT

In April 1994, the Hutu extremist-led government in Rwanda initiated a systematic assault that resulted in the killing of more than 500,000 members of the Tutsi minority in just 100 days. Hate propaganda broadcasted by the infamous Radio Télévision Libre des Mille Collines played a pivotal role in inciting citizens to take part in massacres of their Tutsi and moderate Hutu neighbors. The use of hate speech and calls for violence disseminated through radio were identified as major catalysts of the genocidal violence in Rwanda. Afterwards, executives of this radio station were convicted of genocide and crimes against humanity by a United Nations tribunal. The influence of mass media on this event, as well as on other atrocities, from the Holocaust to genocidal actions in Bosnia, resonates strongly in the present age of digital platforms. Today, every user possesses a potentially powerful global megaphone in the form of their social media profile that, without the proper guardrails, may be used to spread hateful content rapidly and with devastating consequences.

Hate speech and propaganda have thrived in the age of social platforms, where information is being shared at an unprecedented scale

DOI: 10.1201/9781003359982-3

and speed. Unlike in traditional media, online hateful content can be produced at a low cost and shared easily and often anonymously. In addition to fueling toxicity online, which polarizes populations and breaks down norms of trust and social solidarity, hate speech can have stark consequences offline. Some studies have shown a causal link between instances of hate speech online and an increase in violence toward targeted minorities. Yet there is still a debate about the empirical evidence on how hateful online content translates into real-life behavior. Some scholars claim there is rarely evidence that speech alone is causally related to physical violence, while also pointing to the evidence that hate speech, when combined with other factors, may be jointly causing violence and conflict.[1] Others are pointing to the architecture of social media platforms that can affect existing conflict dynamics, worsening existing divisions and fortifying harmful behaviors.[2]

This chapter explores the role of algorithms in spreading hateful content and also presents the potential for machine learning and natural language processing to tackle the problem. Although this chapter covers algorithms and their role in inciting or fighting hate speech specifically, the opportunities and challenges are similar to other uses of machine learning to combat different types of online harm, such as misinformation and disinformation. We will predominantly use examples from Meta's Facebook platform to explain the role of algorithms in inciting violence and fighting against it. Facebook is one of the largest social media platforms in the world; it has by far the largest content moderation operation. It has also come under the most scrutiny for its content moderation decision-making practices, both human and automated. But we will also spotlight efforts outside of Big Tech to positively detect and counter this kind of harmful content.

THE WICKED PROBLEM OF HATE SPEECH

Limiting and countering hate speech is a wicked problem because there is no universally accepted definition of hate speech, and many countries and institutions have adopted their own interpretation of what hate speech entails. To provide readers with a comprehensive understanding of the issue and its ramifications in the algorithmic age, we define hate speech as "any form of communication, be it in speech, writing, images, or behavior, that uses pejorative or discriminatory language or signs to attack a person or group based on their religion, ethnicity, nationality, race, color, descent, gender, or other identity factor."[3] Although the legal definition of hate speech is not strictly defined, social platforms have made efforts to tackle the issue by implementing terms of use and codes of conduct that explicitly limit this kind of speech, providing their own interpretations of hateful content.

Although online hate speech is widely recognized as a societal issue that requires more attention, in the United States, to take one example, what many consider to be hate speech is legally protected under the right to freedom of speech in the Constitution.[4] The lack of clarity around this issue increases the risk of mislabeling the content as hate speech and violating freedom of expression. However, freedom of expression can also be subject to limitations to ensure that it does not infringe on the rights of others. Therefore, some research suggests focusing instead on "dangerous speech" as a narrower and more specific category, defined not by hatred as a subjective emotion but by its capacity to inspire harm. Dangerous speech is any form of expression that can increase the likelihood that its audience will condone or commit violence against members of a particular group.[5]

ALGORITHMS AS PART OF THE PROBLEM OF SPREADING HATE SPEECH

Social media platforms have become a vital part of our lives. According to the 2022 findings, 4.62 billion users around the world are active on social media, which is about a 10 percent increase over the last year.[6] YouTube has 2.1 billion monthly active users worldwide, and 122 million users per day, while users spend around 250 million hours on the platform every day.[7]

People spend around 20 percent of their time online, and users today consume more news and information from social media than from traditional news organizations.[8] Social media is a major source of news, particularly for young people, and around half of all adults in the United States use social media for news. As Facebook grew, so did hate speech and other toxic content on the platform—as well as its ability to detect it.[9] In 2022, the combination of AI and human detection resulted in Facebook proactively taking action on millions of hateful content items every month. Nonetheless, an independent observer found that, every day, 3 million Facebook posts are flagged for review by 15,000 Facebook content moderators, while the ratio of moderators to users is one to 160,000—a scale that suggests that the human content moderators cannot hope to keep up.[10]

Probably the most devastating example of social media involvement in hate-related political violence in recent years was the 2017 violence in Myanmar. The abuse of the internet to spread hateful and dangerous narratives and explicit calls for violence contributed to atrocities perpetrated by the Myanmar military against the Rohingya people.[11] In 2018, the chairman of the UN Independent Fact-Finding Mission on Myanmar reported that social media, particularly Facebook, had played a "determining role" in the human rights violations committed against the Rohingya population by spreading disinformation and hate speech.[12] Posts containing hateful content were made before, and months after, state-led violence displaced 700,000 Rohingya Muslims and tortured and killed tens of thousands, in what the UN has described as genocide. Analysis revealed that some of the most hateful posts gained thousands of reactions and were shared up to 9,500 times, while Facebook took no action to remove this content for months.[13] The impact of such easy creation and sharing of hateful content becomes even graver in the specific context of Myanmar, where Facebook was equated with the internet for many.[14]

In order to grasp the complexities of this situation, it is crucial to acknowledge that the absence of Unicode-compatible font encoding for languages in Myanmar played a significant role in hindering the deployment of automated tools to detect harmful content. Myanmar relied on a different system known as Zawgyi as the dominant typeface for encoding Burmese language characters.[15] This lack of standardization around Unicode made automation and proactive detection of violating content much harder.[16] This technical issue was only solved in 2020, enabling greater use of AI in automated content detection in Myanmar.

As highlighted by Frances Haugen, the Facebook whistleblower, in her 2021 testimony to US senators, the situations in Myanmar and more recently in Ethiopia are only the "opening chapters of a story so terrifying, no one wants to read the end of it."[17] Haugen testified how Facebook's algorithm was provoking ethnic violence by picking up extreme sentiments and divisions. She noted that these posts attracted high engagement, while Facebook struggled to adequately identify dangerous content and lacked expertise in many local languages, including those spoken in Myanmar or Ethiopia. Amnesty International's 2022 report specifically called out Facebook, accusing its algorithms of "proactively amplifying" anti-Rohingya content.[18]

Hate speech incidents online have been reported in almost every country across the globe, including in democracies such as the United States and the United Kingdom, which have been experiencing a rise in misinformation and hate speech, especially online. The wave of white nationalist and anti-democratic rhetoric spreading on social media (as well as other media outlets) in the United States in 2021 culminated with a violent attack on the Capitol.[19] In 2019, the New Zealand mosque shooting, which claimed the lives of 49 Muslims at prayer, was broadcasted on YouTube, with attempts to replicate the video 1.5 million times on Facebook within 24 hours of the attack (Facebook was able to block 1.2 million of these videos at upload).[20] In India, communal violence often originates from rumors spread on WhatsApp groups. In Sri Lanka, in 2019, rumors spread online led to ethnic violence, prompting the government to block access to Facebook, WhatsApp, and Viber in response. The ongoing conflict in Ukraine is witnessing another wave of hateful content from both sides, with platforms struggling yet again to implement uniform content moderation decisions—temporarily allowing calls for violence against Russian occupiers as an expression of support for Ukraine.[21]

Today, social media platforms employ various machine-learning tools to rank the content we see in search results and news feeds (ranking systems) and to make recommendations on news and content to consume as well as products to buy (recommender systems). Machine-learning algorithms differ from traditional algorithms, as the former are trained on data to learn correlations instead of being hard-coded by engineers. This training process allows the algorithm to become a machine-learning model, which can then automate future decisions based on the correlations learned. Social media platforms use algorithms to show users content that is likely to be of interest to them based on their past activity on the platform. The more similar a user's interests are to the interests of the one who is posting the information, the more likely they are to be recommended that specific post. While this can be helpful in suggesting relevant content, it can also be a tool for amplifying hate speech and other harmful content.

One way machine-learning models can spread hateful content is through "engagement-based" prioritization. Essentially, posts that generate more likes, comments, and shares are shown to more users. Unfortunately, this means that controversial content often generates more engagements, which is how hateful speech may be prioritized over less controversial content. Another way algorithms can spread hateful content is through "recommendation-based" prioritization. In this case, the platform recommends content to users based on what it thinks they will be interested in.

This can create "echo chambers" and "filter bubbles" of specific conversations, niche topics, and often extreme viewpoints, where users are exposed mainly to content that reinforces their existing beliefs and may not have much exposure to counterarguments or alternative views. Examples are numerous, from Myanmar, India, Sri Lanka to Ethiopia, Kenya, Germany, the United States, and many more. An older example of this phenomenon includes a leaked document from 2016, which showed Facebook at the time was not only hosting a large number of extremist groups but also promoting them to its users, with 64 percent of all instances of joining an extremist group being due to Facebook's recommendation tools.[22] More recent research, however, suggests that filter bubbles are probably not driving polarization and its short-term impact on the average individual; at the same time, social media does impact the broader population and can contribute to conflict escalation dynamics.[23]

Following frequent accusations of rewarding hateful and provocative content, Facebook has implemented systems to decrease the distribution of sensational, misleading, or false content (discussed in greater detail in the next section). However, despite these efforts and significant investments in AI and machine learning, Facebook's machine-learning capabilities for content moderation still face challenges, particularly in smaller countries experiencing conflict and ethnic divisions.

The surge in hate speech on Facebook during the 2020–2022 civil war in Ethiopia, which has been linked to acts of violence, indicates that the company's efforts are not foolproof.[24] For instance, after a prominent Ethiopian singer advocating for better treatment of the Oromo ethnic group was assassinated, Facebook was flooded with hate speech and incitements to violence that reportedly led to some 150 Ethiopians losing their lives.

In addition to criticism of not removing hateful content promptly, social media platforms have faced criticism when their automated tools have resulted in the erroneous takedown of content posted by human rights activists seeking to document war atrocities or human rights violations. Social media content posted by perpetrators, victims, and witnesses of abuses has become increasingly important in the prosecution of war crimes, and the permanent removal of such content by moderators or an AI-enabled system can hinder efforts to bring those responsible to justice. Human rights groups and activists have been advocating for social media platforms to set up independent mechanisms to safely archive this material "for use in national and international investigations, as well as for research by nongovernmental organizations, journalists, and academics."[25]

The issue of "algorithmic amplification" has prompted a plethora of regulatory proposals worldwide, with the aim of holding tech companies liable for content promoted by their recommendation systems, removing engagement-based content ranking, or giving users an option to "turn off" their algorithms and return to a chronological news feed. Several larger platforms have publicly committed to upholding the Guiding Principles on Business and Human Rights, and introduced various systems of self-regulation, moderation, or oversight mechanisms—although gaps in transparency and implementation still exist.[26]

The European Centre for Algorithmic Transparency (ECAT) was established in 2023 in the European Union to improve understanding of how algorithms powering online platforms and online search engines work.[27] It will assess specific risks and propose new approaches to algorithmic transparency and best working practices. Most recently, in a policy brief leading up to the 2024 Summit of the Future at the United Nations, the UN secretary-general proposed a code of conduct for information integrity on digital platforms, requesting more investment in human and AI content moderation systems in all languages.[28] Some researchers, however, argue that the solution is not outside of the algorithms but building better algorithms. They are working on an alternative to an approach mostly used by social media platforms today that tends to highlight the most attention-grabbing content.

ALGORITHMS AS FORCES TO STOP, NOT SPREAD, HATRED AND VIOLENCE

Since the Myanmar violence at least, social media platforms have been working to address the growing issue of online hate speech through the development of "integrity" systems that go beyond just content moderation. Facebook has acknowledged its own failures and has taken steps to address them, including increasing investments in content moderation and fact-checking partnerships, improving their algorithmic systems, hiring more language experts, and working with Google and the government of Myanmar to transition from Zawgyi to Unicode so content can be detected, routed for review, and moderated. Other social media platforms have also come under scrutiny—and been compelled to adapt—for their role in spreading and amplifying dangerous speech in conflict-affected countries like Sri Lanka, South Sudan, Ethiopia, and Ukraine. Even as clear gaps and failures remain evident, these actions have likely prevented massive amounts of harmful content from being widely shared (although we may never know how much).

Social media platforms have implemented or strengthened many techniques to combat the spread of hate speech, including content moderation by both human moderators and automated tools such as machine learning algorithms to detect and remove harmful content and enforce appropriate pre-existing content rules and guidelines. Human content moderators can be responsible for verifying whether reported content is harmful and making judgments on the removal of such content.

A big challenge, though, is that the ever-increasing amount of user-generated content makes it difficult for human moderators to manage. Furthermore, human moderators must continuously process an ever-growing amount of often distressing content, resulting in significant mental health costs and potential severe trauma.[29] As a result, the strengthening of algorithmic systems for detecting harmful content and AI-powered content moderation has become increasingly important, addressing the slow, laborious, and often harmful nature of this inherently responsive model of human moderation.

Algorithms are trained to identify what is acceptable and what is not on a particular platform, following that platform's standards for content and use, enabling them to automatically analyze and classify potentially harmful content. Compared to humans, AI-powered systems excel in their ability to handle the sheer volume of user-generated content, drastically increasing the speed and efficiency of the overall moderation process. Furthermore, real-time content moderation can also be implemented, with harmful cases potentially automatically detected before they go live.

FACEBOOK'S APPROACH TO LIMITING HATE SPEECH

Hate speech is not allowed under Meta's Community Standards.[30] In response to growing pressure from governments and the public to take down violent and harmful content more quickly, Facebook has invested heavily in AI tools that can proactively flag posts that are potential violations of its standards.[31] Facebook's hybrid approach to content moderation involves automated tools as the first layer, with human moderators stepping in when an algorithm is uncertain. If algorithms determine that the content in question clearly violates Facebook's Community Standards, they may remove it automatically without passing it on to a human moderator.[32]

The platform also employs AI in multiple ways to detect memes and graphics that violate its policies. Such content is then added to a photo database so that similar posts can automatically be deleted. Additionally, AI is utilized to identify word clusters that might be used in a hateful and offensive manner. Meta is also tracking how these clusters change over time and geography to proactively address local trends in hate speech. As a result, harmful content that is rapidly going viral can be swiftly removed.

According to Meta, when there is an increased risk of harm, the company may adopt a more aggressive approach. For instance, according to Meta, "ahead of elections and during periods of heightened unrest in India, Myanmar, and Ethiopia, we significantly reduce the distribution of content that likely violates our policies on hate speech and incitement of violence while our teams investigate it. Once it is confirmed that the content violates these policies, we remove it."[33] In countries that are susceptible to conflict, Meta may also demote potentially inflammatory content to mitigate the risk of it "spreading rapidly or inciting violence and hatred, taking local context into account."[34]

Moreover, when it finds instances of users who have a pattern of posting violating content, Meta says that it makes significant efforts to minimize the distribution of this content, in addition to the standard practice of removing accounts that frequently violate Community Standards. In certain situations, the distribution of possibly violating content may be minimized, even when Meta's systems predict that a particular post has a "very low probability" of violating their policies. This measure is taken while responsible teams investigate the matter. Difficulties in adjudicating some of these decisions led Meta to establish an independent Oversight Board in 2020 to review and make final decisions on some of the most difficult content moderation cases.[35]

Once online hate speech is identified, determining the appropriate course of action poses a multifaceted challenge, not just for Facebook but for numerous other digital platforms. Some other platforms may choose to completely remove the offending content, such as posts, comments, images, and videos, if it violates their policies on hate speech. Alternatively, if the content is still offensive or harmful to users but does not violate platform policies, it may be marked with a warning label, allowing users to make an informed decision on whether to view it. Some platforms may also reduce the visibility of the content, such as by placing it lower in search results or reducing its reach on the platform's algorithmic feed. Depending on the severity of the violation, some platforms may warn the user—or even ban their account and monitor activity to ensure they are not engaging in further hate speech. Finally, companies can also "deplatform" users who have violated their rules, thereby removing spreaders of hate speech. This more extreme step, some argue, has the potential to backfire as it could lead to fears of censorship and bias, therefore deepening polarization, and simply drive bad actors to spaces that are more difficult to monitor.

As these examples show, in spite of the power of AI, human beings remain fundamentally important in making judgments about content. This is because hate speech is highly context-sensitive, often playing in the gray areas of language. Machines are still not capable of making the kinds of contextual and nuanced judgments that are often needed to identify hateful content. As an example, during the pandemic, to address the lack of human reviewers due to lockdowns that did not allow them to physically come to work, Facebook and other platforms predominantly delegated content moderation to algorithmic systems. However, at that stage, algorithms proved to be insufficient tools for the automated removal of hateful and fake content, mostly lacking the capability to distinguish between content that breaks or follows the company's rules.[36] In Syria, where journalists rely on social media to document potential war crimes, numerous activists' accounts were abruptly closed due to automated decisions, frequently without a chance to appeal. On the other side, some questionable content remained online, like in France, where "campaigners fighting against racism and antisemitism noticed a more than 40 percent increase in hate speech on Twitter, with less than 12 percent of those posts being removed."[37]

DEEP DIVE: HOW MACHINE LEARNING IS USED FOR HATE SPEECH DETECTION

As mentioned above, hate speech can often be difficult to identify. In this section, we describe in detail the approaches and challenges when using models of content classification through machine learning techniques. Machine learning refers to a process where an algorithm is trained on training data to identify patterns in data sets. The resulting models can then be applied to new data sets to detect similar patterns. By using machine learning models like natural language processing, hate speech can (theoretically) be automatically detected.

Natural language processing is a subarea of machine learning that processes vast amounts of data in natural language. It is the latest state-of-the-art technique that can perform different tasks such as sentiment analysis, text generation, classification, and questions and answers. The natural language processing field experienced significant growth in late 2018 after Google researchers introduced BERT (Bidirectional Encoder Representations from Transformers), a new language model available under an open-source license. Since then, new language models inspired by the transformers have been developed, demonstrating substantial results in various applications. To be useful in a specific context, language models need to be fine-tuned and adapted for a particular task. In the case of hate speech detection, the language model needs to be fine-tuned with a set of labeled examples of hate speech.

To collect examples of hate speech, online open sources can be used, and they can be annotated by marking whether hate is present in a given sentence based on a specific set of rules. After collecting enough examples, the language model needs to be fine-tuned to learn how to classify hate speech from previously marked examples. The last step of the training is testing and validation. However, each of these phases presents certain technical and ethical challenges, related to privacy, bias, representation, explainability, and more.

Despite recent advancements in language AI, algorithmic tools are still struggling to grasp the context of specific instances of hate speech, as the same words can have different meanings depending on the context. Machine learning models struggle to understand irony or satire or distinguish between actual hate speech and the use of words to describe hate speech that someone witnessed or wants to expose. These models also struggle to recognize intentional typos, which are often used by malicious actors to deceive the model. Researchers have also noted that even simple things like adding the word "love" to instances of hate speech can cause them to go undetected by models.[38] To highlight the scale of the false-positive problem, consider a scenario where an algorithm can detect certain information with 99.995 percent accuracy and thus has a false-positive rate of only 0.005 percent. This means that out of the more than 1 million pieces of content produced on Facebook each day, 15,000 would be falsely flagged, which could have detrimental consequences for freedom of expression.[39]

In a research study, scientists interviewed experts in civil society who deal with online hate speech and developed a taxonomy of 18 different types of hate speech, such as derogatory speech, slurs, and threatening language. They also identified 11 scenarios that AI moderators commonly misinterpret as hate speech, including the use of profanity in innocuous statements, slurs reclaimed by the targeted community, and denouncements of hate that quote or reference the original hate speech. They created an open-source database of more than 4,000 examples, which was used to test two hate speech detection systems: Google Jigsaw's Perspective API and Two Hat's SiftNinja.[40] The test revealed that the systems either failed to detect variations and moderated too little, or moderated too much and censored non-hateful content, reclaimed slurs, and counterspeech.

Presumably, much of this can be addressed, for example, by training the models to adapt to known behaviors of malicious actors, as well as by vastly expanding the quality and size of the language data sets that the models are using. In the past, the data sets for many languages have been quite small in comparison to English, but these are rapidly expanding. Yet language is constantly evolving, and so is hate speech. Regardless of how advanced our technological solutions become, such as creating new models, expanding data sets, and including multiple languages, automated interventions may always be limited in their ability to capture the full range of nuances and complexities of language.

Thus, the only way to overcome some of these limitations is to continue to rely on human moderators to make the final decision in many instances. Ultimately, it is important for any approach to have a clear strategy to address the likely abundance of false negatives and false positives in hate speech monitoring.

OTHER TECH SOLUTIONS

Innovations are also taking place outside of the big social media platforms by organizations that wish to increase understanding of the problem and identify potential solutions. Hate speech can serve as an early warning indicator, prompting some organizations to utilize social media data and insights to track changes in public sentiment in real time and take early action against violence and hate crimes. By understanding how the prevalence of hate speech is changing over time, it may be possible to quantify the degree to which violence and atrocities are rising or falling in a particular place and time—which can help decision-makers allocate attention and resources to places that need it most.

This is the premise that The Sentinel Project used to start its Hatebase Project, the world's largest online repository of structural multilingual hate speech, spanning 95 languages and 175 countries.[41] It uses natural language processing to detect, monitor, and analyze hate speech across the globe, with the goal of identifying it early and preventing its escalation into violence. Sentinel has utilized hate speech as an early warning indicator of violence to inform its projects in Kenya, Myanmar, and the Democratic Republic of the Congo.

PeaceTech Lab, in partnership with Media Monitoring Africa, has created a lexicon of hate speech that is used for semi-automated monitoring of both online and offline media.[42] The process involves analyzing offensive and inflammatory language directed at individuals or groups based on ethnicity, religion, race, gender, national identity, or political affiliation, which has the potential to escalate into violence. This initiative produced biweekly reports that predict potential violence on the ground, which are then compared with the monitoring of hate speech. A predictive model was developed that uses publicly available historical data sets to forecast trends for the upcoming week. While the project does not establish causal relationships, it identifies trends and correlations between speech and violence.

The UK government developed a machine learning hate speech detection tool to automatically detect Islamic State propaganda videos on social media platforms.[43] The tool used machine learning algorithms to analyze the visual and audio content of the videos and compared it to a database of known terrorist propaganda so that the propaganda content can be blocked before it is uploaded online. This approach is highly controversial, creating the risk of censoring free speech flagged as hate speech. Another concern is that it could be used to unfairly target and monitor certain groups or individuals. Additionally, there are concerns about the effectiveness of the tool, as it may not be able to keep up with the constant evolution of propaganda techniques used by extremist groups.

Google's Jigsaw has developed Perspective—a free API that harnesses the power of machine learning to detect toxic comments by scoring their perceived impact on conversation.[44] The team started by collecting millions of comments on the internet and annotating each one according to whether they were deemed toxic. Using these annotated data sets, models were trained to predict the level of toxicity based on the examples provided. These models were thoroughly tested in various scenarios before being released to publishers and platforms for use, who are invited to provide feedback and expand the data set. This system utilizes algorithms to preemptively flag the content as potentially toxic to its creator before it is published. It also assists moderators by alerting them promptly about potential violations of community guidelines.

In order to effectively address the harmful effects of hate speech, it is crucial to address the underlying technological and social factors that contribute to extremist behavior online. This is where, potentially, counterspeech or counter-messaging has a role as a way of engaging in hate-filled conversations to restore civil, less polarized discourse.[45] With hate speech becoming more prevalent online, it is necessary to move beyond traditional physical spaces and find ways to bring counterspeech and conflict resolution methods into digital spaces. The Dangerous Speech Project is a research initiative that explores the causes and impacts of dangerous speech and offers guidance on countering hate speech in various regions, including Nigeria, Sri Lanka, Denmark, Hungary, Kenya, Pakistan, and the United States, through methods such as counterspeech.[46]

Another way of bringing peacebuilding strategies into the digital space is through exploring the application of restorative justice principles in social media moderation and hate speech monitoring.[47] This approach has been developed at the University of California,

Berkeley, with the goal of offering a set of principles for platform moderation that reflect restorative justice practices. Rather than solely punishing offenders by removing their content and accounts, which is the primary approach of social platforms currently, this approach centers on repairing harm and promoting healing for both individuals and the community as a whole.[48]

Some organizations are taking a unique approach to combating hate speech by redirecting it toward resources, education, and support groups that can mitigate it. Moonshot is leading the way in this effort by utilizing data and algorithms to create positive connections instead of fueling hate and violence.[49] By combining a digital footprint with advice from social workers and former extremists, Moonshot develops algorithms to assist in risk assessments of violent extremism online. Once individuals who are at risk are identified, Moonshot interacts with them and provides alternatives to their views, choices, and narratives. Essentially, Moonshot is repurposing advertising algorithms for social good, offering individuals the chance to speak with a counselor—instead of promoting a new product to buy.

LESSONS LEARNED AND WAY AHEAD

While AI has the potential to play a bigger role in dealing with hate speech online, it is important to understand that it comes with a set of challenges and risks. One issue is that most of the research that has been done so far has only considered content written in English or other major languages. However, many malicious activities are happening in other languages. Additionally, not all hateful content is produced and disseminated only in textual format. More research needs to be concentrated on other content forms, such as images and videos. AI trained to spot hate speech is primarily trained by text and still images, which means that video content, especially live content, is "much more difficult to automatically detect as possible hate speech."[50] Another challenge is the decision of many platforms to keep their data access closed or hard to obtain, even for research purposes.

While algorithms can be useful in identifying questionable content quicker and at scale, human moderators are still essential for handling complex cases, understanding context, and making more nuanced decisions. Looking ahead, advancements in natural language processing, content monitoring, creating data sets in diverse languages, and increased transparency and cooperation among digital platforms can potentially drive progress and make online spaces safer. Ultimately, the fight against hate speech will likely require both technological advancements and human engagement to address these complexities effectively.

Finally, we want to stress that, as of the writing of this chapter, there is another possible amplifier of hate speech that has gained significant momentum. As generative AI gains popularity and companies rush to incorporate it into their products, concerns have been raised about the ethics of this technology. ChatGPT has become the fastest-growing consumer application in history, reaching 100 million monthly active users in January 2023.[51] Soon after Open AI released its latest GPT-4 version, Microsoft integrated ChatGPT with its Bing search engine, while Google released its own AI competitor, Bard. These AI tools are impressive in terms of their speed and power, with GPT-4 having 1 trillion parameters, compared to GPT-3's 175 billion. However, this has also increased the risk of them becoming super spreaders of disinformation and other harmful content.[52]

In 2020, researchers at the Center on Terrorism, Extremism, and Counterterrorism at the Middlebury Institute of International Studies found that GPT-3 could be used to produce content written in the style of mass shooters, generate fake forum threads discussing Nazism, and create extremist text in multiple languages. Recent reports and research have highlighted the fact that generative AI tools have been responsible for producing disinformation and hate speech, convincingly presenting such content to users as if it were factual.[53]

Before releasing GPT-4, OpenAI hired a "red team" to adversarially test GPT-4, searching for ways to expose potential harms and problems.[54] Examples of potentially harmful prompts ranged from identifying and locating purchasable alternatives to chemical compounds needed for producing weapons, writing hate speech, and helping users buy unlicensed guns online. These and other efforts will be necessary to prevent GPT-4 and other generative models from being weaponized by malicious actors to manufacture disinformation and hate speech campaigns that are potentially far more destructive than those currently occurring on social media.

NOTES

1 Catherine Buerger, "Speech as a Driver of Intergroup Violence: A Literature Review," *Social Science Research Network*, April 26, 2022, https://doi.org/10.2139/ssrn.4066876.

2 Helena Puig Larrauri and Maude Morrison, "Understanding Digital Conflict Drivers," in *Fundamental Challenges to Global Peace and Security*, ed. Hoda Mahmoudi, Michael H. Allen, Kate Seaman (Palgrave Macmillan, 2022, 169–200).

3 "What Is Hate Speech?" *United Nations*, accessed 11 November 2022, https://www.un.org/en/hate-speech/understanding-hate-speech/what-is-hate-speech.

4 "Freedom of Speech," *Stanford Encyclopedia of Philosophy*, May 1, 2017, accessed July 2, 2023, https://plato.stanford.edu/entries/freedom-speech/#MilHarPriHatSpe.

5 "Dangerous Speech: A Practical Guide," *Dangerous Speech Project*, April 19, 2021, https://dangerousspeech.org/guide/.

6 Rem Darbinyan, "The Growing Role of AI in Content Moderation," *Forbes*, June 14, 2022, https://www.forbes.com/sites/forbestechcouncil/2022/06/14/the-growing-role-of-ai-in-content-moderation/?sh=3b79aca74a17.

7 Luke Munn, "Angry by Design: Toxic Communication and Technical Architectures," *Humanities and Social Sciences Communications* 7, Article number: 53 (July 30, 2020), accessed December 2, 2022, https://doi.org/10.1057/s41599-020-00550-7.

8 Fernando Chirigati, "Fighting Hate Speech and Misinformation Online," *Nature Computational Science* 2, 281–283, May 1, 2022, accessed December 5, 2022, https://doi.org/10.1038/s43588-022-00238-9.

9 Sheera Frenkel, Nicholas Confessore, Cecilia Kang, Matthew Rosenberg, and Jack Nicas, "Delay, Deny and Deflect: How Facebook's Leaders Fought through Crisis," *The New York Times*, November 14, 2018, https://www.nytimes.com/2018/11/14/technology/facebook-data-russia-election-racism.html.

10 Tyler Adkisson, "Artificial Intelligence is Now Used to Track Down Hate Speech," *Scripps News*, August 11, 2022, accessed February 22, 2023, https://scrippsnews.com/stories/artificial-intelligence-is-used-to-track-down-hate-speech/.

11 Sarah Oh and Zachary Nelson, "The Incomplete Digital Transformation - Countering online hate and its offline consequences in conflict-fragile settings," *SSRN Electronic Journal*, February 9, 2023, https://doi.org/10.2139/ssrn.4353001.

12 Tom Miles, "U.N. Investigators Cite Facebook Role in Myanmar Crisis," *Reuters*, March 12, 2018, https://www.reuters.com/article/us-myanmar-rohingya-facebook/u-n-investigators-cite-facebook-role-in-myanmar-crisis-idUSKCN1GO2PN.

13 Megha Rajagopalan, Lam Thuy Vo, and Aung Naing Soe, "How Facebook Failed the Rohingya in Myanmar," *BuzzFeed News*, August 28, 2018, accessed March 9, 2022, https://www.buzzfeednews.com/article/meghara/facebook-myanmar-rohingya-genocide.

14 Victoire Rio, "The Role of Social Media in Fomenting Violence: Myanmar," *Toda Peace Institute*, Policy Brief No:78, June 2020, accessed July 2, 2023, https://toda.org/policy-briefs-and-resources/policy-briefs/the-role-of-social-media-in-fomenting-violence-myanmar.html.

15 Juan Cebu, "Unified under One Font System as Myanmar Prepares to Migrate from Zawgyi to Unicode," *Rising Voices*, September 7, 2019, https://rising.globalvoices.org/blog/2019/09/06/unified-under-one-font-system-as-myanmar-prepares-to-migrate-from-zawgyi-to-unicode/.

16 Nick LaGrow and Miri Pruzan, "Integrating Autoconversion: Facebook's Path from Zawgyi to Unicode," *Engineering at Meta*, September 26, 2019, https://engineering.fb.com/2019/09/26/android/unicode-font-converter/.

17 "Facebook is under New Scrutiny for its Role in Ethiopia's Conflict," NPR, October 11, 2021, https://www.npr.org/2021/10/11/1045084676/facebook-is-under-new-scrutiny-for-its-role-in-ethiopias-conflict.

18 "Myanmar: Facebook's Systems Promoted Violence against Rohingya; Meta Owes Reparations," *Amnesty International*, September 29, 2022, https://www.amnesty.org/en/latest/news/2022/09/myanmar-facebooks-systems-promoted-violence-against-rohingya-meta-owes-reparations-new-report/.

19 Rory Cellan-Jones, "Tech Tent: Did Social Media Inspire Congress Riot?" *BBC News*, January 8, 2021, https://www.bbc.com/news/technology-55592752.

20 "1.5 Million Videos of Christchurch Mosque Attack in New Zealand Removed by Facebook," *France 24*, March 17, 2019, https://www.france24.com/en/20190317-new-zealand-mosque-attack-videos-facebook-ardern.

21 Emerson T. Brooking, "Meta Meets the Reality of War," *Technology and Democracy* (blog), *Tech Policy Press*, March 15, 2022, https://techpolicy.press/meta-meets-the-reality-of-war/.

22 Karen Hao, "The Facebook Whistleblower Says Its Algorithms Are Dangerous. Here's Why," *MIT Technology Review*, October 5, 2021, https://www.technologyreview.com/2021/10/05/1036519/facebook-whistleblower-frances-haugen-algorithms/.

23 Jonathan Stray, Ravi Iyer, and Helena Puig Larrauri, "The Algorithmic Management of Polarization and Violence on Social Media," *Social Science Research Network*, May 25, 2023, https://doi.org/10.2139/ssrn.4429558.

24 Zecharias Zelalem and Peter Guest, "Why Facebook Keeps Failing in Ethiopia," *Rest of World*, November 13, 2021, https://restofworld.org/2021/why-facebook-keeps-failing-in-ethiopia/.

25 Fred Abrahams, "When War Crimes Evidence Disappears: Social Media Companies Can Preserve Proof of Abuses," *ReliefWeb*, May 25, 2022, https://reliefweb.int/report/ukraine/when-war-crimes-evidence-disappears-social-media-companies-can-preserve-proof-abuses.

26 See UN Guiding Principles at the Business sand Human Rights resource Center, https://www.business-humanrights.org/en/big-issues/un-guiding-principles-on-business-human-rights/.

27 See European Commission website for initiative European Centre for Algorithmic Transparency, accessed July 1, 2023, https://algorithmic-transparency.ec.europa.eu/index_en.

28 "Our Common Agenda Policy Brief 8 Information Integrity on Digital Platforms," *United Nations*, June 12, 2023, https://www.un.org/sustainabledevelopment/blog/2023/06/our-common-agenda-policy-brief-8-information-integrity-on-digital-platforms/.

29 Casey Newton, "The Trauma Floor - The Secret Lives of Facebook Moderators in America," *The Verge*, February 25, 2019, https://www.theverge.com/2019/2/25/18229714/cognizant-facebook-content-moderator-interviews-trauma-working-conditions-arizona.

30 See more about Facebook's Hate Speech Policy at Facebook's Transparency Center https://transparency.fb.com/policies/community-standards/hate-speech/?source=https%3A%2F%2Fweb.facebook.com%2Fcommunity standards%2Fhate_speech.

31 Samidh Chakrabarti and Rosa Birch, "Understanding Social Media and Conflict," Meta, June 20, 2019, https://about.fb.com/news/2019/06/social-media-and-conflict/.

32 "Facebook Community Standards," *Meta*, accessed July 3, 2023, https://transparency.fb.com/policies/community-standards/?source=https%3A%2F%2Fwww.facebook.com%2Fcommunitystandards%2F.

33 Miranda Sissons, "Our Approach to Maintaining a Safe Online Environment in Countries at Risk," *Meta*, October 23, 2021, https://about.fb.com/news/2021/10/approach-to-countries-at-risk/, accessed July 5, 2023.

34 Samidh Chakrabarti and Rosa Birch, "Understanding Social Media and Conflict," Meta, June 20, 2019, https://about.fb.com/news/2019/06/social-media-and-conflict/.

35 See Sissons, "Our Approach to Maintaining a Safe Online Environment in Countries at Risk," and "Ensuring respect for free expression, through independent judgment," *Oversight Board*, accessed July 2, 2023, https://oversightboard.com/.

36 Mark Scott and Laura Kayali, "What Happened When Humans Stopped Managing Social Media Content," *Politico*, October 21, 2020, https://www.politico.eu/article/facebook-content-moderation-automation/.

37 Ibid.

38 Tommi Gröndahl, Luca Pajola, Mika Juuti, Mauro Conti, and Nadarajah Asokan, "All You Need Is 'Love': Evading Hate-Speech Detection," arXiv: 1808.09115, November 5, 2018, accessed November 7, 2022, https://arxiv.org/abs/1808.09115.

39 Brittan Heller, "What Mark Zuckerberg Gets Wrong—and Right—about Hate Speech," *Wired*, May 2, 2018, accessed June 19, 2023, https://www.wired.com/story/what-mark-zuckerberg-gets-wrongand-rightabout-hate-speech/.

40 Paul Röttger et al, "HateCheck: Functional Tests for Hate Speech Detection Models," Proceedings of the 59th Annual Meeting of the Association for Computational Linguistics and the 11th International Joint Conference on Natural Language Processing, pages 41–58, August 1–6, 2021, accessed April 22, 2023, https://aclanthology.org/2021.acl-long.4.pdf; and Karen Hao, "AI still sucks at moderating hate speech," *MIT Technology Review*, June 4, 2021, https://www.technologyreview.com/2021/06/04/1025742/ai-hate-speech-moderation/.

41 See more at the Sentinel Project website, https://thesentinelproject.org.

42 "Putting the Right Tools in the Right Hands to Build Peace," *Peace Tech Lab*, accessed May 12, 2023, https://www.peacetechlab.org/.

43 Natasha Lomas, "UK Outs Extremism Blocking Tool and Could Force Tech Firms to Use It," *TechCrunch*, February 13, 2018, https://techcrunch.com/2018/02/13/uk-outs-extremism-blocking-tool-and-could-force-tech-firms-to-use-it/?guccounter=2#:~:text=The%20Home%20Secretary%20has%20today.

44 "Machine Learning Can Help Reduce Toxicity, Improving Online Conversation," *Jigsaw*, accessed June 19, 2023, https://jigsaw.google.com/the-current/toxicity/countermeasures/.

45 Joshua Garland, Keyan Ghazi-Zahedi, Jean-Gabriel Young, Laurent Hébert-Dufresne, and Mirta Galesic, "Countering Hate on Social Media: Large Scale Classification of Hate and Counter Speech," *ArXiv:2006.01974*, June 5, 2020, https://arxiv.org/abs/2006.01974.

46 See Dangerous Speech Project at https://dangerousspeech.org/.

47 "A Restorative Justice Approach to Social Media Moderation," *UC Berkeley School of Information*, July 1, 2020, https://www.ischool.berkeley.edu/news/2020/restorative-justice-approach-social-media-moderation.

48 Amy A. Hasinoff, Anna D. Gibson, and Niloufar Salehi, "The Promise of Restorative Justice in Addressing Online Harm," *Brookings*, July 27, 2020, https://www.brookings.edu/techstream/the-promise-of-restorative-justice-in-addressing-online-harm/.

49 See Moonshot website at https://moonshotteam.com/.

50 Tyler Adkisson, "Artificial Intelligence is Now Used to Track down Hate Speech," *Scripps News*, August 11, 2022, https://scrippsnews.com/stories/artificial-intelligence-is-used-to-track-down-hate-speech/.

51 Krystal Hu, "ChatGPT Sets Record for Fastest-Growing User Base - Analyst Note," *Reuters*, February 2, 2023, https://www.reuters.com/technology/chatgpt-sets-record-fastest-growing-user-base-analyst-note-2023-02-01/#:~:text=Feb%201%20(Reuters)%20%2D%20ChatGPT.

52 "Despite OpenAI's Promises, the Company's New AI Tool Produces Misinformation More Frequently, and More Persuasively, than its Predecessor," *NewsGuard's Misinformation Monitor*, March 2023, accessed May 12, 2023, https://www.newsguardtech.com/misinformation-monitor/march-2023/.

53 "Google's New Bard AI Generate Lies," *Center for Countering Digital Hate*, April 5, 2023, https://counterhate.com/research/misinformation-on-bard-google-ai-chat/#about, and "Disinformation Researchers Raise Alarms about A.I. Chatbots," *The New York Times*, February 8, 2023, https://www.nytimes.com/2023/02/08/technology/ai-chatbots-disinformation.html.

54 "OpenAI's Red Team: The Experts Hired to 'Break' ChatGPT," *Financial Times*, April 14, 2023, https://www.ft.com/content/0876687a-f8b7-4b39-b513-5fee942831e8.

3

AI, HUMAN RIGHTS, AND PEACE

MACHINES AS ENABLERS OF RIGHTS WORK

In the past 15 years, satellite images have been used to detect mass graves in Burundi, detect Boko Haram activities in Nigeria, and in support of the case against Sudanese President Omar al-Bashir at the International Criminal Court for abuses in Darfur. There are even more recent examples in Ethiopia and Ukraine. Adding AI to these use cases is changing the game. We see an increasingly strong potential to combine, on the one hand, AI-enabled technologies (like high-quality satellite imagery), deep learning, and other recent advances in computer science that have transformed how we extract information with, on the other, legal expertise and the work of front-line human rights defenders. As in other domains, we can expect AI to potentially have a transformative impact on human rights work, which is one reason why some human rights organizations, such as Amnesty International, have created specific programs to harness AI.

Not all the news regarding AI and human rights is positive, of course. In the previous chapter, we surveyed the role of AI-driven algorithms in spreading hate and fueling offline violence, including human rights abuse. More generally, there has been important attention to how AI is being used for all sorts of applications that are

DOI: 10.1201/9781003359982-4

undermining fundamental rights (such as privacy and the freedoms of speech and peaceful assembly), enabling surveillance states (using the internet of things, biometrics, facial recognition), and replicating human biases and discriminatory behaviors (for example, in criminal profiling and administrative decision-making). These uses can also create difficulties for peaceful societies and for managing conflicts before they escalate to violence.

This chapter focuses on human rights as defined through existing international agreements, such as the Universal Declaration of Human Rights. It should be noted, however, that AI has also called into question some of the fundamental categories and assumptions that shape human rights discourse. Which entities have the right to have rights in the first place? Why should humans have rights but not, say, animals or AIs?[1] Philosophers often define what is distinctive about human beings through the recognition that humans have both intelligence and consciousness. That said, why couldn't AIs have rights when non-conscious entities like corporations already can? We are just now at the beginning of reframing fundamental questions about "the human" that are destabilizing our categories and reshaping our world.[2] These deeper discussions will undoubtedly change our frameworks for understanding peaceful and rights-respecting societies in the decades to come.

This chapter, however, focuses more narrowly on the potential for using AI for positive human rights outcomes, with an accent on conflict-affected contexts. We begin by briefly summarizing some of the most salient human rights issues relating to peace. To follow, we highlight ways in which AI is already being used as a support to human rights work as a tool in human rights investigations and on specific issues, using the example of slavery and human trafficking (which are relevant in conflict situations, such as the use of child soldiers). We conclude by identifying practical ways that a human rights approach can be deployed to improve the use of AI, as well as summarizing risks and limitations, especially in conflict-affected countries.

HUMAN RIGHTS AND PEACE

We include a chapter on human rights in this book because rights are directly relevant to peace. Indeed, human rights norms came to be codified following World War II as a response to both the causes and the horrors of war. The Universal Declaration of Human Rights (1948) specifically had peace as one of its aims, and a founding idea was to limit the power of states to infringe upon fundamental freedoms that all people should have to foster more peaceful societies. Since the Universal Declaration, which described civil/political rights (e.g., rights to free speech and association) as well as social/economic rights (rights to work, health, etc.), many treaties have created a broad legal framework to ensure a range of rights.

Specifically, there are several ways we can see the link between human rights and peace. First, the violation of human rights (e.g., systemic discrimination on the basis of gender or ethnicity, targeted killings, or mass censorship) is a strong signal that a country is not peaceful. Indeed, when rights are violated systematically or at a large scale—whether by the state or by other groups— a society is often already in conflict or on the brink of conflict. Recall our many examples in the previous chapter from Rwanda, Ethiopia, and elsewhere. Second, human rights protections are themselves building blocks for resilience to violent conflict. Where governments respect the basic rights of *all* citizens—including civil and political rights but also social, economic, and cultural rights— societies show more solidarity and the ability to resolve the normal conflicts that arise in any society. The power of these human rights protections can work both before and after a conflict—helping to prevent a country from falling into violence as well as helping it emerge from it after a war.

Finally, human rights require that there should be a remedy for their violation, which is important for building trust and solidarity in a peaceful society—especially when that trust has been broken due to repeated violations.

AI AND THREATS TO RIGHTS

We have all seen the examples on the news: countries using surveillance technologies to crack down on protestors, censor dissenting views, monitor and intimidate critics of the government, and restrict people's movements. One of the biggest stories for AI and human rights is the growing risk of AI-enabled surveillance states in which fundamental freedoms are regularly restricted.

The fear of an overpowering surveillance state is nothing new. In East Germany during the Cold War, such a state operated through the low-tech means of neighbors surveilling and informing one another. And around the same time that Alan Turing was inventing the computer in the 1940s, George Orwell imagined the surveillance state through the metaphor of "Big Brother" in his dystopian novel, 1984.

What is new is the massive growth of data of all kinds and the use of AI to quickly learn from the data and detect patterns. Much criticism has focused on the use of surveillance technologies by closed states, such as China's "Great Firewall" to monitor the internet and the use of biometrics and facial recognition to monitor protestors in Hong Kong in 2019. But the fact is that many, if not most, states are using AI-enabled technologies for some surveillance purposes in one form or another, at national and local levels. As a well-known example, police departments in the United States have used facial recognition software that has been found to have racial biases (due to algorithms trained to recognize mainly white European faces) to identify perpetrators of crimes—resulting in false arrests. The problem of surveillance that invades privacy and restricts freedom is more spectacular in some countries than others, but it is a widespread—not isolated—phenomenon.

Pervasive state surveillance is a threat to rights, but so are administrative uses of AI to help make decisions about everything from welfare benefits to hiring to creditworthiness. Observers note that there is not enough due diligence done before AI is integrated into administrative decision-making, which can lead to negative outcomes, including the invasion of privacy and discrimination based on gender, ethnicity, and other categories.[3]

Finally, AI-driven algorithms, as described in the previous chapter, have enabled the spread of hate speech, misinformation, and disinformation. These actions create polarization in civil society that disrupts the ability for rational debate in the public space. When citizens' arguments (and deep beliefs) are based on misinformation, deep fakes, and hateful and dehumanizing stereotypes, the risk of tipping into conflict is greater.

All of the above is directly relevant to peace, as peaceful societies are ones in which citizens can trust the decisions of their government (and have a transparent understanding of why the decisions were taken), where they can exercise basic freedoms without threats of imprisonment or harm, and where rational debate about what constitutes a good society is possible.

AI AS AN ENABLER FOR HUMAN RIGHTS AND PEACE

As mentioned, our main objective in this chapter is to highlight the innovations that are taking place with respect to AI and human rights—especially as these are not as well known. One of the features that makes AI so powerful is its ability to make visible what is usually hidden or invisible. Human rights abuse is usually something that countries and perpetrators do everything they can to hide from detection, precisely because they worry about being held to account.

While the opportunities are many, we focus on uses that demonstrate a clear added value to human rights protection work: scaled-up ability to detect and document abuses; the capacity to better combat specific abuses, such as human slavery and trafficking; and improved access to information and productivity gains.

HELP WITH HUMAN RIGHTS INVESTIGATIONS AND DOCUMENTATION

There are several ways in which AI-enabled technologies are already advancing investigation and detection efforts, especially with new forms of remote sensing data, like satellite and drone images.

Technological advances, particularly in the last two decades, have enabled the identification of abuses through human review of satellite images showing labor camps or forced displacement, for example, or by citizen uploads of videos documenting people being arrested, beaten, or even killed. What AI has begun to enable in these instances is working with much larger bodies of video, images, and other kinds of data to show patterns that would be too difficult for individual human monitors to identify on their own. While the use of this kind of evidence may still be limited in the courtroom, it can still have significant value in publicizing abuse and ultimately forcing countries and judiciaries to take cases seriously, as we saw with the video footage showing the murder of George Floyd in the United States.

Amnesty International has been one of the leaders in this space with their Citizen Evidence Lab. In Mexico, they have combined machine learning and geospatial analysis to aid local groups in their efforts to find missing and disappeared persons. For example, they used supervised machine learning techniques to narrow the search area around already-identified clandestine graves, where there was a greater probability of finding additional grave sites.[4] They have also conducted analysis of human rights–related violence in Myanmar (2017) and Darfur (2021) using an algorithm that identifies hot spots for fires from satellite imagery.[5]

Another emerging application is more complex: developing full visual reconstructions of events out of a myriad of videos and other sources—since it is rare for a single video to capture the entirety of an event. Forensic Architecture, in collaboration with SITU Research, led efforts nearly ten years ago to reconstruct events in Gaza that involved a military response to the kidnapping of an Israeli soldier. Working with Amnesty International, the partners collected videos, images, satellite imagery, and testimonies from eyewitnesses and journalists to create a 3D model of Rafah, then synchronizing all of this to a universal clock. This effectively mapped evidence in time and space as a way of analyzing how events unfolded from a range of perspectives.[6] However, most of this time-consuming and painstaking work was done manually. Machine learning/computer visioning promises to make this work much more efficient.

Products are currently in the pipeline to help. A relevant example comes from the Center for Human Rights Science at Carnegie Mellon University, which has developed applications to combine machine learning and computer vision with larger sets of visual data. Researchers have created a tool called Event Labeling Through Analytic Media Processing (E-LAMP) that can analyze large sets of videos to detect classifiers—which may be visual, aural, semantic, or a combination of the three—and perform speech recognition in English and Arabic. The Center is working with human rights partners on applications to ultimately help tag large video collections that can be used for investigative and analytical purposes.[7]

Indeed, E-LAMP was invited to help reconstruct protest events in Ukraine in 2013–14, which resulted in police killings and injuries. Specifically, it was asked to develop methods for synchronizing the large number of videos that were taken of the protests where abuse occurred. Researchers then developed an algorithm to identify specific features that appeared across the videos (for example, the sound of wind, screaming, gunshots, or airplane noise) that could be used to synchronize the videos.[8] They emphasize, however, that in the end, the results of algorithms still must be reviewed by humans, with synchronizations checked manually to ensure accuracy.

While this is just a small sample of current initiatives, it demonstrates the promise in this space. There are difficulties and limitations as well. One being the fact that the validity of AI-assisted efforts as evidence in a courtroom is still in question, and another being that most organizations, especially local ones, do not have the required expertise or scale to undertake this kind of analysis as yet. Finally, as generative AI continues to improve, we expect there will be a proliferation of deep fake images that will start to shake the credibility of visual evidence to its core. Although there are AI-driven algorithms for identifying deep fakes, and digital forensics has a growing toolbox, it is unclear if the countermeasures for detection of fakes will be able to keep up with the rapid advances in generative AI.[9]

Finally, there are ways that AI-enabled technology might help human rights investigations—but some wonder if the risk is too great or the ethics too murky to use them. For example, in Ukraine, concerns were raised about the use of Clearview AI's facial recognition technology, which was offered to the government free of charge to help identify the dead (to notify loved ones) or reunite families. Identifying the missing and giving closure to loved ones is an essential part of human rights work, in addition to accountability for abuses. But in this case, human rights advocates warned that the government was playing with fire by using technology that is generally used for surveillance and for curtailing rights. Indeed, some worry that this positive use of facial recognition is being used publicly to "whitewash" the more insidious uses of facial recognition in the country.[10]

TACKLING SPECIFIC ABUSES: MODERN SLAVERY AND TRAFFICKING

Let us now take a deeper look at a specific use case for AI. Modern slavery, including human trafficking, forced labor, and child labor, is not a relic but a fact of life for more than 40 million people in the world (as of 2021).[11] In fact, every single country in the world "hosts" men, women, and children trapped in slavery. Part of the problem is often the hidden nature of modern slavery, leading to the inability to recognize vulnerabilities and vulnerable populations early on.

Machine learning is now providing methods to use traditional and novel data streams to model environments at high risk as well as vulnerable groups and individuals, and for the first time, to do that at scale. Lack of data or lack of good quality data is often an obstacle for conducting machine language projects. To address this challenge, N/Lab modern slavery researchers at the University of Nottingham used features extracted from inexpensive proxy data—such as mobile phone data sets, drone imagery, and demographics—to find relationships between these variables and other accurately labeled, but very expensive, examples of "ground truths" of modern slavery incidents. In this way, they have been able to model vulnerability for modern slavery among different groups, to provide evidence for targeted anti-slavery efforts.[12]

Some populations are especially at risk and vulnerable—those who live in countries impacted by wars and conflicts. Modern slavery occurs in 90 percent of recent wars and conflicts (as of 2020). The most common type of enslavement in war zones is the use of child soldiers, which occurs in 87 percent of armed conflicts.[13] To tackle this problem, the Dallaire Institute for Children, Peace, and Security has piloted the Knowledge for Prevention project, which aims to provide early warnings to better protect children in conflict environments. The project created the first data set on evidence of recruitment and developed a predictive model, incorporating child-centered indicators, to raise awareness of the risks of recruitment at an early age and inform better and more effective prevention measures.[14]

Not all technology applications to end slavery are without controversy. Like the example of Ukraine and Clearview AI mentioned above, the use of AI-powered facial recognition technologies in particular is a highly contested issue. Marinus Analytics, a company that was awarded third place at the famous IBM Watson AI XPRIZE competition, used AI-powered analytics tools and big data that save hours and days of investigative time to find traffickers and recover victims. The company was one of several organizations allowed to continue using Amazon's Rekognition tools, which were otherwise put on a moratorium for police use due to their controversial applications and bias against people of color and minorities, with civil society and advocacy groups demanding a permanent ban.[15] In conflict and post-conflict areas, this application is even more controversial, especially with refugee communities, where many are fleeing persecution; using their facial and biometric features could make them an easy target for governments with nefarious aims.

ACCESS TO INFORMATION AND IMPROVED PRODUCTIVITY

Human rights defenders rely on the law—essentially, text—to make claims and to defend rights. There is a voluminous body of international and domestic law, as well as an ever-increasing number of relevant reports on human rights from national human rights bodies, regional organizations, as well as the international human rights architecture, which is centered around the United Nations. Widely available automated translation tools, like Google Translate, are already making these documents much more accessible.

While this may not be the most exciting application of AI, the reality from a practical standpoint is that the use of natural language processing and the availability of a sophisticated ChatGPT tool promise to substantially reduce the time and effort required for human rights defenders to find relevant legal standards, access and synthesize documents, and create the best cases possible. As one example, the organization Human Rights Information and Documentation Systems (HURIDOCS) has been working with a human rights group that focuses on the UN's Universal Periodic Review—a process that every country in the world goes through every five years to help improve its performance on human rights issues—a process that generates voluminous text that makes it difficult for human rights advocates to find the things they need. With help from Google.org, HURIDOCS has used BERT and TensorFlow to create a classifier to categorize all the human rights recommendations that emerge from this process, which are then submitted for human review. This has reduced the time it takes to classify documents for each cycle from two to three months to just one week.[16]

Additionally, as has been well-reported in the media, the legal field has been an early adopter of ChatGPT, especially for providing the initial research basis for cases. Of course, human review is still necessary to avoid mistakes—for example, the case in which ChatGPT hallucinated fake legal citations, which a lawyer tried to use in court.[17]

For voluminous visual evidence, VFRAME provides additional machine learning tools to help in the process of verifying information. Mnemonic, which is an organization dedicated to documenting war crimes and human rights abuse based in Berlin, has been using VFRAME in its verification and classification pipeline for media archives collected from credible sources in places like Syria and Yemen.[18] Since 2017, the Yemeni Archive has gathered visual media from journalists, citizens, and open-source videos from social media platforms. The team uses machine learning to detect the use of banned cluster munitions being used on civilians in the conflict.[19] It is estimated that it would take a person many years to search through this information—which machine learning reduces to around 30 days. UNITAD has used machine learning tools to scour video for images of explosions, grave digging, and other evidence of atrocities.[20]

HOW HUMAN RIGHTS CAN MAKE AI BETTER

Not only can AI be an enabler for human rights work, but human rights can also create models for better and more rights-sensitive AI. A fundamental idea is that all AI—and especially "AI for good" and AI in the public interest—should adhere to human rights standards and have a solid understanding of its human rights impacts. Indeed, human rights can provide a set of guardrails to protect individuals and communities from harmful uses of AI.

This has become a hot topic in recent years, both in the public and private sectors, as stories about AI's use leading to violations of privacy and biased decision-making have proliferated.

Governments from the United States to the European Union (EU) have also taken steps. The EU has issued specific guidance on "future-proofing human rights in the age of AI." It calls for more information and transparency about how AI is being used in administrative decision-making, as well as public consultations about implementation. It asks that human rights impact assessments be conducted *before* AI solutions are implemented. The Netherlands, which is a member of the EU, has mandated such impact assessments for all public institutions as of 2022, with indicators to assess whether algorithms violate particular rights and freedoms.[21] It also demands that its member states adopt legal standards to address human rights violations related to AI in the private sector. There is a worry that the voices of corporations get too much attention in the discussion on AI and that companies are too often left to self-regulate rather than adhere to agreed standards.

For the private sector, a central guidepost is the UN Guiding Principles on Business and Human Rights, which were launched in 2011. Within the tech domain, Meta is a notable example of a company that has made efforts to put some of these principles into practice. They hired a Director of Human Rights in 2019 and, as mentioned in the previous chapter, have developed a company-wide Human Rights Policy. Additionally, Meta has issued an annual human rights report and investigated its own impact in places like Israel/Palestine, Cambodia, and Myanmar. While many observers are critical of this self-reporting, it suggests that Meta has been moved by external pressure to engage differently on human rights issues, at a minimum.

Since 2019, however, even industry leaders have started to call for more government regulation of AI. In 2023, the EU created an overarching legal framework called the AI Act—still in draft form at the time of this writing—which would be the first ever legal regulation of AI, if adopted. Amnesty International has argued that the AI Act is critical to "ending the use of discriminatory and rights-violating artificial intelligence (AI) systems."[22] Among other things, the framework promises to limit the use of facial recognition software and prohibit companies from scraping biometric data from social media sites.[23] It also proposes a set of "transparency obligations" that would be required of any generative AI that interacts with humans, is used to detect emotions and social categories, or is used to generate or manipulate content, like deep fakes.[24] The law would require more transparency about how generative AI like ChatGPT works, and it would also insist that content created from chatbots and other generative AI be clearly labeled.

The use of AI for human rights and peace contains its own paradoxes. The very same AI that can be incredibly helpful to human rights defenders may also be contributing to human rights harm. This is why regulation is essential. But finding guardrails that support rather than hinder innovation will be a challenge.

LOOKING AHEAD

The massive growth in and public availability of all sorts of real-time, potential evidence—satellite images, citizen videos, documents, etc.—coupled with the pattern-finding and generative power of AI is putting new tools into the hands of human rights defenders. We close this chapter by re-emphasizing the centrality of human rights to peace and the importance of understanding how AI is affecting rights up and down its creation and user chains. This is because sometimes the *ways* that rights are being affected are surprising.

For example, in response to criticism that their algorithms were pushing radical and violent content to users, social media companies created algorithms to identify and remove such content. However, we now find that a lot of citizen and journalist videos of abuses that could have been useful for documenting human rights violations are being automatically detected and deleted by the big platforms. During the Russian invasion of Ukraine in 2022, a journalist documented a gruesome scene that included families that had been shot dead and burnt-out cars in the suburbs of Kyiv. When he tried to post them on Facebook, YouTube, and Instagram to share with the world, they were all immediately detected and removed. This and many other similar instances have led a member of Meta's Oversight Board to say that the industry has been overcautious in its removal of content.[25]

Another example concerns recent revelations about ChatGPT's production pipeline. To reduce the chances of ChatGPT reproducing violent, hateful, or racist speech in the content it generates (after all, ChatGPT is trained on the internet, which is full of this kind of speech), the company created a safety team and detection algorithms. In order to create the labels of toxic speech for the detection algorithms, the company reportedly turned to underpaid workers in Kenya, where employees were paid on average roughly $2 an hour to label the content—much of it containing highly disturbing imagery, as it was drawn from the darkest reaches of the internet. This raises concerns about global inequality and exploitative working conditions, especially as these workers may have ongoing mental health challenges due to the toxicity of the content they regularly sort through.

Like any technology, AI does not cut only one way; regulation will be essential to making AI a more positive than negative force for human rights and peace. So far, efforts by the tech community to self-regulate, while welcome, are often too reactive and do not always grasp the full range of possible impacts on human rights and peace, especially in rapidly changing conflict environments. We anticipate that the calls for greater transparency, public participation, impact assessments, labeling of generative AI content, and legal rules in line with human rights standards will remain central to human rights advocacy in the coming years.

NOTES

1 See Mathias Risse, "Human Rights and Artificial Intelligence: An Urgently Needed Agenda," *Human Rights Quarterly* 41 (2019): 1–16.

2 See, e.g., William F. Schulz and Sushma Raman, *Why Realities Demand New Rights: The Coming Good Society* (Harvard University Press, 2020).

3 "Human rights by design: future-proofing human rights protection in the era of AI" (Council of Europe, May 2023).

4 Ana Josseline Alegre Mondragón, Fernanda Lobo Diáz, Jorge Luis Reyes, and José Luis Silván Cárdenas "Finding Clandestine Graves: Using Geospatial Analysis to Search for Missing Persons in Baja California, Mexico," June 30, 2022, https://citizenevidence.org/2022/06/30/finding-clandestine-graves-using-geospatial-analysis-to-search-for-missing-persons-in-baja-california-mexico/; accessed June 12, 2023.

5 Micah Farfour, "Using VIIRS Fire Data for Human Rights Research," February 26, 2021, https://citizenevidence.org/2021/02/26/using-viirs-fire-data-for-human-rights-research/; accessed June 12, 2023.

6 See Amnesty International and Forensic Architecture, "'Black Friday': Carnage in Rafah," n.d. https://blackfriday.amnesty.org; accessed June 23, 2023).

Also discussed in Jay D. Aronson, "Computer Vision and Machine Learning for Human Rights Video Analysis: Case Studies, Possibilities, Concerns, Limitations," *Law & Social Inquiry* 43, no. 4 (Fall 2018), 1198–99.

7 Aronson, "Computer Vision and Machine Learning for Human Rights Video Analysis."

8 Ibid., 1204.

9 Stuart A. Thompson and Tiffany Hsu, "How Easy Is It to Fool A.I. Detection Tools?" The New York Times, June 28, 2023, https://www.nytimes.com/interactive/2023/06/28/technology/ai-detection-midjourney-stable-diffusion-dalle.html. See also Agnes E. Venema and Zeno J. Geradts, "Digital Forensics, Deepfakes, and the Legal Process," *The SciTech Lawyer* 16, no. 4 (Summer 2020): 14–23.

10 Alexa Hagerty, "In Ukraine, identifying the dead comes at a human rights cost," Wired, February 22, 2023, https://www.wired.com/story/russia-ukraine-facial-recognition-technology-death-military/; accessed June 23, 2023.

11 International Labour Organization, "Global Estimates of Modern Slavery: Forced Labour and Forced Marriage" (ILO, September 2022).

12 For example, see N-Lab's work in Brazil: N-Lab, "Modelling Vulnerability to Slavery in Brazil," https://www.nlab.org.uk/project/radar/; accessed June 9, 2023.

13 University of Nottingham Rights Lab, "Slavery and trafficking occurs in 90 per cent of recent wars and conflicts, new research shows," October 17, 2020, https://www.nottingham.ac.uk/news/slavery-trafficking-in-90-per-cent-recent-wars-conflicts#; accessed June 9, 2023. See also Contemporary Slavery in Armed Conflict Dataset at https://www.csac.org.uk/; accessed June 9, 2023.

14 See Dallaire Institute, "Early Warning to Early Action," https://www.dallaireinstitute.org/early-warning; accessed June 9, 2023.

15 Tate Ryan-Mosley, "We could see federal regulation on face recognition as early as next week," MIT Technology Review, May 21, 2021, https://www.technologyreview.com/2021/05/21/1025155/amazon-face-recognition-federal-ban-police-reform/; accessed June 23, 2023.

16 See an overview of HURIDOCS's machine learning work, "Human Rights and Machine Learning," https://huridocs.org/initiatives/machine-learning-for-human-rights-information/; accessed June 12, 2023. See also Grace Kwak Danciu, "Unlocking Human Rights Information with Machine Learning,"

December 8, 2021, https://blog.google/outreach-initiatives/google-org/unlocking-human-rights-information-with-machine-learning/; accessed June 12, 2023.

17 Ramishah Maruf, "Lawyer Apologizes for Fake Court Citations from ChatGPT," CNN Business, May 28, 2023, https://www.cnn.com/2023/05/27/business/chat-gpt-avianca-mata-lawyers/index.html.

18 Mnemonic, "Methods," https://mnemonic.org/en/about/methods; accessed June 12, 2023.

19 Karen Hao, "Human rights activists want to use AI to help prove war crimes in court," MIT Technology Review, June 25, 2020, https://www.technologyreview.com/2020/06/25/1004466/ai-could-help-human-rights-activists-prove-war-crimes/; accessed June 12, 2023.

20 The Economist, "AI helps scour video archives for evidence of human rights abuses," June 5, 2021, https://www.economist.com/international/2021/06/05/ai-helps-scour-video-archives-for-evidence-of-human-rights-abuses.

21 "Human rights by design: future-proofing human rights in the era of AI" (Council of Europe/Commissioner for Human Rights, 2023), 11.

22 Amnesty International, "EU: European Union must protect human rights in upcoming AI Act vote," April 26, 2023, https://www.amnesty.org/en/latest/news/2023/04/eu-european-union-must-protect-human-rights-in-upcoming-ai-act-vote/; accessed June 12, 2023.

23 Adam Satariano, "Europeans Take a Major Step Toward Regulating A.I.," New York Times, June 14, 2023; https://www.nytimes.com/2023/06/14/technology/europe-ai-regulation.html.

24 See Proposal for a regulation of the European Parliament and the Council - Laying down harmonised rules on artificial intelligence (Artificial Intelligence Act) and amending certain union acts, COM(2021) 206 final, section 5.2.4.

25 Jack Goodman and Maria Korenyuk, "AI: War crimes evidence erased by social media platforms," BBC.com, June 1, 2023; https://www.bbc.com/news/technology-65755517.

4

AI, CLIMATE, AND CONFLICT

THE ROLE OF DATA SCIENCE IN CLIMATE CHANGE AND SUSTAINING PEACE

Climate change is widely recognized as the paramount crisis of our era and the most pressing challenge humanity faces today. It has resulted in a gradual increase in temperature, rising sea levels, biodiversity loss, ocean acidification, land and forest degradation, and salination. According to the World Meteorological Organization in 2021, the frequency of natural disasters stemming from weather, climate, and water extremes has increased fivefold from 1970 to 2019, accounting for half of all natural disasters during that period. Of the 10 costliest natural disasters in history, seven have occurred since 2000, and all were linked to climate change. In 2023, global warming reached 1.1°C above pre-industrial levels. Without urgent action, the Intergovernmental Panel on Climate Change says it is likely that warming will reach up to 2°C by 2100, leading to irreversible and catastrophic harm to our ecosystem.[1]

Rising temperatures are not only fueling further environmental degradation, natural disasters, weather extremes, food and water insecurity, and economic disruption, but they can also be linked to the likelihood of violence, terrorism, and armed conflict. The impacts

DOI: 10.1201/9781003359982-5

of climate crises can contribute to drivers of conflict and risks to peace and stability, with disproportionate impacts on developing, fragile, and conflict-affected states. The interactions of these many factors are, however, incredibly complex. The advent of big data analytics, which involves the collection and analysis of vast amounts of data, is making a significant impact on scientific research and brings potential for advancements in the field of climate–conflict research. Computer scientists, including those from DeepMind, Google AI, and Harvard, have emphasized the potential applications of machine learning (ML) in addressing climate change—spanning research into climate impacts and adaptation to climate modeling.[2] While ML has been utilized in modeling global climate systems for some time, its application to climate–conflict research is still emerging but holds immense promise.

This chapter aims to raise awareness of the promise and perils of AI for climate–conflict research, to explore new tools for anticipating, preventing, and responding to climate-related conflict, to explore potential for building planet-centered technologies, and to educate more informed climate- and conflict-aware technologists, data scientists, designers, engineers, and technology activists. We begin with a high-level survey of the climate–conflict nexus, followed by a dive into some use cases for AI in research and practice relating to this nexus. We conclude by looking at challenges (including the environmental impact of high-energy-consumption AI models themselves) and the way ahead in this very uncertain—but critically urgent—moment in human history.

THE CLIMATE–CONFLICT NEXUS

The relationships between conflict and climate, although a subject of continuous research, is not a settled issue. While some claim that climate change and global warming can cause conflict, others insist that evidence of causal links is weak. While there continues to be disagreement about the exact relationship between climate change and conflict, there is a stronger consensus that climate *shocks*—sudden and extreme climate events—if not well managed through effective governance and equitable responses, can raise the risk of violent conflict. The idea of climate change as a "threat multiplier" acknowledges that climate can interact with existing political, social, and demographic conditions to amplify communities' security risks.[3]

On a practical level, examples of the relationship between climate change and conflict are numerous. In the Sahel, a region of the Sahara Desert that cuts across many national borders, conflicts between farmers and herders and between different pastoralist groups may hinge on disputes over access to water and land use. These conflicts can be triggered or exacerbated by climate change. In particular, researchers found that "rainfall shocks," such as a decline in rainfall in a given year, are related to a rise in conflict between neighboring communities of farmers and herders. These shocks may force herders to migrate in search of pasture to graze their livestock, resulting in heightened tensions with nearby farmers and—possibly—violence. A typical decline in rainfall for herders, according to this research, can result in a rise in conflict risk in neighboring farm communities by 35 percent—importantly, with no effect on conflict if the same rainfall shock is experienced by a non-herder group.[4] A further piece of research relating to Africa concludes that a 1°C temperature rise generates only a 17% rise in conflict likelihood in communities where these two groups do not co-exist, as compared to a 54 percent rise where both farmers and herders live side-by-side.[5]

In Nigeria, clashes between farmers and herders, particularly in the Middle Belt region, have been fueled by a combination of environmental factors and ethnic tensions.[6] Extreme weather events, increasing desertification in northern Nigeria, high-intensity rainfall in southern Nigeria, and the expansion of farmland into traditional grazing areas have contributed to conflicts over access to land and resources. In Somalia, the prolonged drought, soil erosion, and depleted grazing land have had severe consequences, exacerbating conflict and displacement.[7] Competition over water and pasture for livestock, coupled with failed crops, has aggravated tensions between different groups. This has been further compounded by political instability, weak governance, and the presence of armed groups. In the coastal areas of Bangladesh, rising sea levels and more frequent cyclones pose significant challenges to communities.[8] Displacement and loss of agricultural land due to saline intrusion have triggered conflicts over scarce resources among affected populations, exacerbating social and economic vulnerabilities.

This list is not exhaustive, and many forecast further deteriorations if more is not done to tackle the complexities of the climate–conflict nexus and connect advances in scientific evidence with timely policy change and practical action. Scientific research has provided evidence of indirect causal links between climate impacts, socio-economic pressures, vulnerabilities, and violent conflict.[9] Impacts of climate change can obstruct economic development in conflict-affected countries in which agriculture is the predominant livelihood resource. Inequality, weak governance, and a history of fighting are well-established risk factors for conflict. At the same time, the likelihood of violent conflict is reduced by good governance, strong social protection systems, effective justice systems, and the protection of property rights, among other things.

The influence of climate change on these risk and resilience factors for conflict has been part of research for some time now, but further research on these correlations is necessary to understand the precise nature of these links and guide policymakers in sustaining peace in the time of climate change and natural disasters. However, there are various obstacles to conducting such research, including difficulties in data collection in unsafe and often inaccessible regions and a lack of timely and high-resolution climate and conflict data.

ILLUSTRATIVE USE CASES OF MACHINE LEARNING IN CLIMATE–CONFLICT RESEARCH AND PRACTICE

Conflict data sets, risk models, and early warning systems can be useful tools for grasping the relationship and complexities between climate change and violent conflict. They can inform decision-makers when to act and potentially help save lives. As we explained in the first chapter, researchers and practitioners are using data science and AI to forecast conflict. In the future, these models could incorporate relevant climate and conflict data to enable climate–conflict research. This analysis could better inform the addition of climate dimensions to peacebuilding and humanitarian interventions, as well as help to shape peace programing in places where climate change may be affecting local dynamics. In this section, we survey some of the most promising areas for current and future AI-driven research relating to the climate and conflict.

In general, researchers have already identified several factors that can amplify the effects of environmental stress and increase the likelihood of violence, such as social inequalities, poor governance, and contested access to resources, as well as negative perceptions of other social groups.[10] At the same time, these factors can also be worsened by environmental stress. However, trying to measure these social issues through traditional data collection, such as surveys, can be costly and time consuming. The collection of data on climatic and conflict indicators can be difficult, especially at the sub-national level or in war zones and conflict-affected areas. This is exactly where AI-driven, big data approaches can potentially help.

Research on "vulnerability" offers crucial insights for decision-making on climate change adaptation. It describes the entities and people most vulnerable to climate change, explains the reasons behind their vulnerability, and outlines salient time frames and risk factors. Many gaps in understanding vulnerability still exist, and big data analytics can potentially help to fill these gaps. Automated collection of real-time data, especially in data-poor environments, has the potential to advance research and analysis. Some researchers propose analyzing online discussions, such as Twitter threads, as a method of generating more insights faster. Natural language processing can be used to analyze substantial textual content and make observations about how "vulnerability" factors emerge in discussions about climate change across social media platforms. These insights can potentially reveal shifts in popular opinions and discourse on contentious issues or indicate potential sites of protest or violence.[11] AI-enhanced analysis of social media activity could also reveal relevant socio-political patterns that increase vulnerability to violence in the wake of climate shocks.

Leveraging big data can help create geospatial datasets that include important factors influencing vulnerability, like socioeconomic status, the availability of infrastructure to mitigate harms, or environmental/weather patterns. Geospatial big data—such as high-resolution imagery—can be used to monitor trends, evaluate the risks associated with natural disasters, and analyze settlement patterns in regions prone to high risk. Satellite data can provide insights into weather patterns, temperature variations, and more. It can also be used to identify and track signs of conflict, displacement, destruction of infrastructure, or the movement of military forces. By analyzing changes in satellite imagery over time and combining it with other data sets, big data techniques can help monitor conflict events and assess their impact on the local population and environment.

Turning to specific use cases, although not exhaustive, in the following paragraphs we share some illustrative examples of how AI has been used in climate–conflict research. The first is Weathering Risk, an initiative aiming to ensure that all relevant policies are better informed by evidence-based analysis on climate-change-related security risks.[12] The goal is to foster lasting peace and avert the onset and intensification of conflicts associated with the effects of climate change. The project combines quantitative and qualitative assessments and scenario-based foresight methods to identify short-, medium-, and long-term risks. ML and regression analysis are applied to test and validate the qualitative analysis—identifying trends across certain contexts as well as outliers and additional indicators not captured through qualitative analysis—ultimately revealing which types of direct and indirect climate-related impacts contribute to which types of conflict and insecurity, at different scales, and under which circumstances. It then advises on concrete actions that can be taken to prevent and reduce these risks, the capacities and resources available, and what steps need to be taken to implement recommended actions in different contexts.

As access to water is increasingly affected by climate change, gaining more insights into the role of water-related shocks and environmental stress in future conflict and violence is critical. Recent statistics show that water-linked violence has surged significantly in the past decade, with incidents more than doubling in the past ten years compared with previous decades.[13] One approach to tackling the issues comes from the World Resources Institute (WRI), a global research organization, that uses ML to analyze data on 80 environmental, social, and economic indicators to estimate how increasing pressure on water and other resources might increase conflict risk.[14] WRI has produced an early warning system for armed conflict, predicting the probability of violence in Africa, the Middle East, and Southeast Asia.

As part of a broader partnership, named Water, Peace, and Security, WRI, together with Wetland International, UNESCO, International Alert, and others, is exploring water crises as opportunities for peacebuilding.[15] The aim of Water, Peace, and Security is to turn the vicious cycles of water-based conflict into virtuous cycles of water-based peace and cooperation. Using innovative tools such as ML, this partnership is helping people identify and understand water-related security risks to assist them in making timely, informed, and inclusive action for conflict prevention and mitigation.[16] This project forecasts the potential for violent conflicts related to water issues by integrating climate elements like rainfall and crop failures with political, economic, and social dimensions of risk. It specifically uses random forest, an ML-based method that relies on decision trees, to forecast conflict up to a year in advance in countries affected by water scarcity. The model is not perfect; half of its predictions for emerging conflicts are false positives, meaning instances where conflict was forecasted but did not actually occur. But it also captures 86 percent of future conflicts, successfully forecasting more than 9 in 10 ongoing conflicts and 6 in 10 emerging conflicts.[17] This project offers an open platform where various actors, including governments and international organizations, can identify hotspots for violence and conflict before they escalate.

Academics are also playing an important role in creating and testing new ideas.[18] In 2021, new research was published that used a random forest approach to assess the role of environmental stress on armed conflict risk in Africa. The model incorporated sub-national data on environmental factors, socioeconomic factors, and ongoing conflict, finding that, overall, environmental factors contribute less than socioeconomic factors to predicting conflict events. They also found that climatic indicators may both increase and decrease conflict risk, depending on the location: in Northern Africa and large parts of Eastern Africa, climate change may increase conflict risk, while for West Africa and the northern part of the Sahel, unstable climate conditions may actually reduce conflict risk. The research concludes that using ML approaches to forecast conflict risk is a practical way to gain insight into the complex interaction of climate change and conflict, with direct relevance for policymakers.[19]

The Fragility, Conflict and Violence (FCV) unit at the World Bank is developing a data set that integrates environmental and conflict risks through the application of machine learning techniques. This work aims to map areas where joint climate–FCV risks are highest and demonstrate different profiles of vulnerability. The first part of the project is mapping climate and conflict vulnerability in order to generate vulnerability clusters and create vulnerability profiles. In the second stage, researchers are using machine learning to measure conflict vulnerability and identify locations where the model is successful in predicting conflict and areas where it is not successful in predicting conflict. Finally, case studies are developed to advance knowledge on climate change and conflict.

Another area where ML techniques can make a significant contribution is at the intersection of conflict, climate change, and forced displacement. As discussed in the first chapter, two noteworthy projects, UNHCR's Project Jetson and the Danish Refugee Council's

Project Foresight, employ machine learning to predict the probability of movements of displaced populations. These initiatives represent promising examples of potential advancements in this field. By utilizing predictive analytics based on various data sources, including the economy, conflict levels, climate conditions, governance, and more, similar initiatives have the potential to forecast the likelihood of large-scale forced displacement related to climate shocks. This, in turn, could enable governments and humanitarian organizations to respond earlier and with greater efficiency.

OPPORTUNITIES, CHALLENGES, AND WAYS AHEAD

Application of big data and different forms of AI to the intersection of climate–conflict research has already demonstrated interesting results. New data sources, such as social media content, mobile phone data, and satellite imagery, offer vast and diverse amounts of data relevant for climate–conflict research. They can complement traditional data sources and help overcome challenges of traditional data collection, such as the high costs of data collection or limited coverage of hard-to-reach areas. Different AI techniques can potentially contribute through their ability to see patterns in data that are too vast for human comprehension. However, applying big data and AI to understanding the climate–conflict nexus also presents multiple challenges.

Some challenges are similar to those in the broader field of conflict forecasting discussed in the first chapter, such as data availability, quality, and access. While big data approaches can help fill data gaps, it is crucial to ensure that the data used for analysis is reliable, accurate, and representative. Other challenges are directly related to the nature of ML work: namely, none of the models will ever give 100 percent accuracy, meaning every model will always flag certain percent of false positives and false negatives. Decision-makers, therefore, will always have to decide if they prefer to incorrectly forecast the presence of conflict or its absence. Another challenge that comes with current prediction models is that, with their usual short-term prediction horizon, they are better at informing short-term policy-making and interventions compared to scenarios to help solve long-term challenges. While having some of these limitations, ML models also open up opportunities with their flexible structure, which allows for the inclusion of new insights and new data sources as they become available.

Recently, the energy consumption of AI systems—specifically ML during training and data center energy usage—has come under scrutiny. Some have started to estimate how AI is contributing to more emissions that warm the planet. The precise amount of energy needed to run large models is not yet fully understood, although one recent estimate suggested that Open AI's training of its Megatron-LM language model over nine days consumed nearly three times as much energy as a single US household consumes in a year.[20] Training just one AI model can "emit more than 626,000 pounds of carbon dioxide equivalent, which is nearly five times the lifetime emissions of an average American car."[21] Due to the concerns surrounding the carbon and water footprint of AI models and their overall environmental sustainability, there is growing advocacy for the establishment of power-efficient data centers and the development of ML models that consume less power. Also, further efforts are needed to develop measurement approaches and enable understanding of both direct and indirect AI environmental impacts.[22]

Because of the use of different data sets or data proxies, timescales, geographical scales, sampling bias, and different definitions of violence and conflict, there is yet no scientific consensus regarding the strength of links between climate change and violent conflict. However, there is a growing consensus that climate-related disruptions are increasingly interacting with drivers of insecurity, violence, and conflict, and we need more effective ways of assessing risks and producing more accurate predictive information. As in any other field, big data and ML will not be panaceas for solving this problem. Nevertheless, if employed with caution, these approaches hold promising potential for enhancing our comprehension of the complex interactions between climate and conflict and empowering more informed and effective decision-making processes.

NOTES

1 See "Climate and Weather Related Disasters Surge Five-Fold over 50 Years, but Early Warnings Save Lives - WMO Report," UN News, September 1, 2021, https://news.un.org/en/story/2021/09/1098662; and Intergovernmental Panel on Climate Change, "Climate Change 2023: Synthesis Report," IPCC, 2023, https://www.ipcc.ch/report/ar6/syr/.

2 David Rolnick, Donti, Priya L, Lynn H Kaack, Kelly Kochanski, Alexandre Lacoste, Kris Sankaran, Andrew Slavin Ross, et al. "Tackling Climate Change with Machine Learning," *ArXiv*, 2019, https://arxiv.org/abs/1906.05433.

3 Claire Doyle, "Addressing the Converging Risks of Climate, Insecurity, and Migration in Central America," *New Security Beat*, May 19, 2023. https://www.newsecuritybeat.org/2023/05/addressing-converging-risks-climate-insecurity-migration-central-america/.

4 Nathan Nunn and Eoin McGuirk, "How Climate Shocks Trigger Inter-Group Conflicts: Evidence from Africa's Transhumant Pastoralists," *VoxDev*, April 30, 2021, accessed November 8, 2022, https://voxdev.org/topic/energy-environment/how-climate-shocks-trigger-inter-group-conflicts-evidence-africa-s-seasonal-migrants.

5 Ulrich J. Eberle, Dominic Rohner and Mathias Thoenig, "DP15542 Heat and Hate: Climate Security and Farmer-Herder Conflicts in Africa," CEPR Discussion Paper No. 15542 (CEPR Press: Paris and London, 2023), accessed November 8, 2023. https://cepr.org/publications/dp15542.

6 Amara Nwankpa, "Managing Existential Risk and Climate Resilience: The Case of Nigeria," *Brookings*, March 14, 2022, https://www.brookings.edu/blog/africa-in-focus/2022/03/14/managing-existential-risk-and-climate-resilience-the-case-of-nigeria/.

7 "As Climate Change Strains Somalia's Path to Peace, Communities Hold the Key," *ReliefWeb*, July 14, 2022, https://reliefweb.int/report/somalia/climate-change-strains-somalias-path-peace-communities-hold-key.

8 Mubashar Hasan and Geoffrey Macdonald, "How Climate Change Deepens Bangladesh's Fragility, *United States Institute of Peace*, September 13, 2021, https://

www.usip.org/publications/2021/09/how-climate-change-deepens-bangladeshs-fragility.

9 Katharine J. Mach, Caroline M. Kraan, W. Neil Adger, Halvard Buhaug, Marshall Burke, James D. Fearon, Christopher B. Field, et al. "Climate as a Risk Factor for Armed Conflict," *Nature* 571 (2019): 193–197, https://doi.org/10.1038/s41586-019-1300-6.

10 Nina von Uexkull, Mihai Croicu, Hanne Fjelde, and Halvard Buhaug, "Civil Conflict Sensitivity to Growing-Season Drought," *Proceedings of the National Academy of Sciences* 113 (44): 12391–12396, October 17, 2016, https://doi.org/10.1073/pnas.1607542113.

11 Ryan Compton, Craig Lee, Jiejun Xu, Luis Artieda-Moncada, Tsai-Ching Lu, Lalindra De Silva, and Michael Macy, "Using Publicly Visible Social Media to Build Detailed Forecasts of Civil Unrest," *Security Informatics* 3 (Article number:4), 2014, https://doi.org/10.1186/s13388-014-0004-6.

12 "The Weathering Risk Methodology," *Weathering Risk*, accessed December 5, 2022, https://www.weatheringrisk.org/en/publication/weathering-risk-methodology.

13 "Water Conflict," Pacific Institute, January 14, 2023, https://www.worldwater.org/water-conflict/.

14 See World Resources Institute website at https://www.wri.org/, accessed December 15, 2022.

15 See Water, Peace and Security website at waterpeacesecurity.org, accessed December 15, 2022

16 Ibid.

17 "Global Early Warning Tool," *World Resources Institute*, accessed July 5, 2023, https://www.wri.org/initiatives/water-peace-security-partnership/global-early-warning-tool.

18 Jannis M Hoch, Sophie P de Bruin, Halvard Buhaug, Nina Von Uexkull, Rens van Beek, and Niko Wanders, "Projecting Armed Conflict Risk in Africa towards 2050 along the SSP-RCP Scenarios: A Machine Learning Approach," *Environmental Research Letters* 16 (12): 2021, https://doi.org/10.1088/1748-9326/ac3db2.

19 Ibid.

20 Mark Labbe, "Energy Consumption of AI Poses Environmental Problems," *TechTarget*, August 26, 2021. https://www.techtarget.com/searchenterpriseai/feature/Energy-consumption-of-AI-poses-environmental-problems.

21 Karen Hao, "Training a Single AI Model Can Emit as Much Carbon as Five Cars in Their Lifetimes," *MIT Technology Review*, June 6, 2019, https://www.technologyreview.com/2019/06/06/239031/training-a-single-ai-model-can-emit-as-much-carbon-as-five-cars-in-their-lifetimes/.

22 "Measuring the Environmental Impacts of Artificial Intelligence Compute and Applications – The AI Footprint," November 2022, OECD Digital Economy Papers, https://doi.org/10.1787/7babf571-en.

5

AI, PEACE, AND ETHICS

FROM PRINCIPLES TO PRACTICE

In the summer of 2023, one of the big global blockbusters was the film *Oppenheimer*, which portrays the fraught period during World War II when human beings created the atom bomb. Many in the media—including the filmmaker Christopher Nolan—have compared this historical moment to our current situation with the emergence and rapid growth of AI. Indeed, fears of nuclear proliferation and debates about the potential global nuclear disaster after World War II echo some of today's discussions around the risks of AI. In 1953, US President Dwight Eisenhower proposed a global agreement to prevent the spread of nuclear weapons while also sharing peaceful uses of nuclear technology for energy, agriculture, and medicine.[1] Although not a perfect mechanism, the proposal did create a pathway for nuclear facilities to be controlled and inspected, including the establishment of the International Atomic Energy Agency and ultimately the creation of the Treaty on the Nonproliferation of Nuclear Weapons, as building blocks of a future nuclear nonproliferation regime. Some ethicists believe we are at a similar moment today, in which a new AI age is demanding a similar framework for governing AI.

DOI: 10.1201/9781003359982-6

Until (and if) such a mechanism is created, users need to commit to an ethical AI for peace. In an era of rapidly advancing technology and heightened conflict and violence, it is crucial that we comprehend the effects of these technologies on those impacted by conflict. Furthermore, we must create and apply ethical solutions that help to prevent violent conflict, reduce human suffering, promote peace, and safeguard citizens, especially those who are most vulnerable. It is also important to take precautions to avoid unintended consequences. The success or failure of sustaining peace with advanced data tools, the possibility of stopping malicious use and unintended consequences, and ensuring accountability all depend on a commitment to embedding ethics into work by design as a natural first and continuous step in developing, designing, and deploying these tools—rather than as an afterthought to be dealt with after the deployment.

The latest advancements in AI can bring transformational change to peace, justice, and human rights. At the same time, they pose some complex ethical questions and challenges linked to issues ranging from bias to data protection to data colonialism in countries with active conflicts or at risk of conflict.

Previous chapters have highlighted key challenges for ethics. One issue is bias: AI systems are only as good as the data they are trained on; therefore, if the data contain biased information, the results will also be biased and lead to unfair outcomes. For example, predictive policing and the use of facial recognition technology in models drawing on historically biased data have already led to wrongful arrests.[2] If conflict early warning systems are trained with incomplete or biased data, they can lead to inaccurate predictions and recommendations, meaning some countries may be marked as false negatives and their populations left without needed early assistance.

We have also discussed hate speech, misinformation, and disinformation. The use of AI in generating and spreading bad information can contribute to the manipulation of public opinion and exacerbate social tensions, including the spread of dehumanizing hate speech and the escalation of conflict. If an AI system for automated hate speech detection uses inaccurately labeled data, the system can wrongly flag and remove certain content as hate speech and violate the freedom of expression, or alternatively leave the hateful content online and amplify the harm.

Ultimately, the use of AI in peacebuilding and conflict prevention may raise questions about the legitimacy of the decision-making process and the trustworthiness of the recommendations provided by the system. This chapter highlights both general and specific challenges for the use of AI for peacebuilding. While there are another whole set of ethical challenges relating to the application of AI in warfare (already tackled through the work of the International Committee of the Red Cross [ICRC], among others), often centering around autonomous weapons systems, our book focuses on applications of AI for sustaining peace—not military uses.[3] This chapter gives an overview of key challenges for AI ethics from a peacebuilding perspective; surveys existing AI principles and guidelines for safe, ethical, transparent AI applications; and suggests how these can be implemented in the peacebuilding field. This chapter also sheds light on existing ethical standards and practices in the traditional (pre-digital) peacebuilding field and proposes ideas on how these tools can be applied by AI experts as well.

ETHICAL RISKS OF AN "AI FOR PEACE" APPROACH

Peacebuilding ethics and humanitarian standards and principles predate digital and AI ethics. Peacebuilding ethics work concentrates mostly around normative issues relating to questions such as: Who has agency in peacebuilding? What ends should peacebuilding pursue, and with what means? Should the international community engage in peacebuilding, and to what extent?[4] "Humanitarians are required to be impartial, independent, professionally competent, and focused on preventing and alleviating human suffering."[5] An AI for peace approach to ethics is, however, only now emerging, and it is distinct from peacebuilding or humanitarian ethics. It aims to provide an understanding of the specific intersection of data science, technology, and peacebuilding and its consequences for peace. It aims to encompass projects that directly aim at sustaining peace, as well as those that have indirect consequences for peace.

Numerous AI ethics resources out there can be helpful, but they can also be overwhelming for peacebuilding organizations, which are often under-resourced in their work and operate under difficult conditions. Also, the basic knowledge and understanding of AI ethics concepts and tools is uneven among different stakeholders—while a minority are experts and even creators of some of these tools, the majority is still lacking basic AI literacy, even when they are part of teams working on AI-driven peace projects. The same gap exists with data scientists operating in the field, who may not have a solid understanding of conflict drivers, familiarity with the context they are operating in, or knowledge of the populations they are trying to help. Despite the mass of AI ethics principles and guidelines now being published, there are few publications covering the ethics of AI for peace, as well as a gap in specific AI ethics tools designed with peacebuilding practitioners as the end-users.

Unfortunately, there are many ethical risks involved in using AI for peace. Some have already been highlighted in previous chapters, while others are new. We briefly sum them up here.

DATA RESPONSIBILITY

Much of the work in AI for peace ethics centers around setting and applying data responsibility standards and practices—given the unprecedented rates of data being collected, data being more accessible online, and data becoming more usable in machine learning. Obtaining good-quality data can be challenging in conflict and fragile settings, as data is scarce, often incomplete, or simply unavailable. Data is often available in various formats (structured and unstructured, digital and analog), which creates additional barriers to its use. Some of the most often discussed data and AI ethics concerns are the risk of bias—coming from incomplete or unrepresentative data fed into a model, which reproduces, reinforces, and amplifies patterns of marginalization and discrimination—and risks to privacy. While some biases occur in the data collection stage, others follow along the data science lifecycle. The ICRC Handbook on Data Protection provides guidance for how to protect and process humanitarian data. It includes five basic principles: fairness and limited processing, purpose limitation, proportionality, data minimization, and data quality.[6]

PRIVATE SECTOR ENGAGEMENT

Private sector engagement in conflict and fragile settings is another ethical dilemma, where private sector collaboration with humanitarian or peacebuilding organizations comes with substantial privacy and civil rights implications. While peacebuilding and humanitarian organizations are increasingly reliant on digital data and third-party partnerships to collect and process it to create impact, the ethical frameworks for doing it responsibly are often not in place, such as policies and procedures for ensuring the application of ethical principles and human rights standards. These projects may come with the risk of repurposing the knowledge gained from one context to another without adequate consideration of the specific vulnerabilities of groups, as well as the risk that data will be used by governments that do not have the interest of affected people on their minds.

One such example was the case of the partnership between Palantir and the United Nations World Food Programme (WFP), which aimed to help WFP use its data to streamline the delivery of food and cash-based assistance in life-saving emergency relief operations around the world, including in conflict-affected countries.[7] Palantir's previous work with police, US military and security agencies, and the wider intelligence community raised concerns about this partnership. Although personally identifiable information was not collected through this cooperation, many observers highlighted the risks of demographically identifiable information being collected and potentially leading to harm to targeted groups. While public-private partnerships have a great value in assisting operations in fragile and conflict contexts, every data-driven project must promise to do no harm to digital and physical safety, human rights, and privacy—especially when it comes to some of the world's most vulnerable people.

DATA WEAPONIZATION

The risk of data weaponization—the use of data to target vulnerable individuals and communities—appears especially grave in conflict and fragile situations. What we saw in 2021 in Afghanistan, after the Taliban takeover, was a growing concern that the Taliban could use social media, online information, or other forms of data to identify citizens who previously worked for the Afghan security forces, civilian government, or foreign and international organizations.[8] Google had temporarily locked down an unspecified number of Afghan government email accounts, protecting the digital trail left by former officials and their international partners.[9] Similarly, in 2022, in Ukraine, Google temporarily disabled Google Maps' live traffic data due to the risk of it being misused as a tool to track military movements and civilians seeking shelter.[10]

DATA MANIPULATION

Data manipulation—the practice of altering or manipulating data—is an especially high risk in fragile settings, where it can be used to further political agendas, spread misinformation, or manipulate public opinion. In the pre-algorithm era, data manipulation was used to misrepresent statistics on violence and war casualties, exaggerate the strength of warring parties, or intimidate and dehumanize enemies. In the age of algorithms, data manipulation may be conducted on a greater scale, amplifying the potential impact of misuse. New data-driven methods can be used to create false content, corrupt the integrity and content of digital datasets, or manipulate the functioning of algorithmic systems.

AI-powered tools can be used to automatically generate large amounts of misleading or false content, manipulate public opinion, or create mistrust of other published information. With the latest developments in deep learning neural networks and a growing number of AI tools built on large language models like ChatGPT, disinformation researchers are raising alarms about AI chatbots spreading conspiracy theories and misleading content. Predecessors of ChatGPT have already been used to infuse online content with misinformation and, often, hate speech. For example, Microsoft had to close out its Tay chatbot within 24 hours of introducing it on Twitter in 2016 after trolls taught it to stream racist and xenophobic language.[11]

AI experts caution that another AI-generated form, deepfakes—artificial but hyper-realistic video, audio, and images—will play a significant role in future elections and broader politics, undermining trust.[12] In 2019, a video purporting to show the president of Ghana taking a bribe went viral on social media.[13] The video was a deepfake, created using AI to superimpose the president's face onto that of another person. The video was intended to undermine the president's credibility and legitimacy, and some feared that it could contribute to political instability or even a coup. In a more recent example, with the beginning of war in Ukraine, a video emerged in public that appeared to show Ukrainian President Volodymyr Zelensky calling on the citizens of his country to stop fighting and surrender their weapons.[14] It was another example of a deepfake mimicking a real person in what appeared to be an authentic video.

DATA LEAKS AND CYBERATTACKS

Data leaks and cyberattacks are risks present in any field, but an especially serious one for fragile settings with vulnerable populations. In

February 2022, a sophisticated cybersecurity attack launched against computer servers hosting information held by the ICRC compromised the personal data and confidential information of more than half a million vulnerable people, including displaced persons separated from their families due to conflict, migration, natural disasters, missing persons, and their families, and people in detention.[15] Cyberattacks can also disrupt critical services, such as healthcare, emergency response, and communications networks. In conflict settings, where these services are already strained, disruptions can have severe consequences and put even more lives at risk.

DUAL-USE APPLICATIONS

The rapid development of AI is prompting worries about its dual-use application, in which any new AI innovation might be used for both beneficial and harmful purposes. In a recent effort to point out the dangers of AI dual use, researchers showed the ease of using computational drug design software to generate novel toxic molecules.[16] It took less than six hours for drug-developing AI to invent 40,000 potentially lethal molecules for possible chemical or biological warfare. In addition to malicious use, some AI applications come with "unintentional harms" or "unintended consequences", where approaches designed with the intent to sustain peace and prevent conflict cause harm but instead exacerbate conflict and violence. Additionally, AI systems often operate in opaque and complex ways, making it difficult to determine who is accountable for their decisions, which is an important issue in sustaining peace and conflict prevention.

NEGLECT AND DISEMPOWERMENT OF LOCAL ACTORS AND COMMUNITIES

The increasing dependence on AI in program design and implementation runs the risk of neglecting localization and community participation—although these are central practical and ethical commitments for peacebuilders.[17] Remote teams, sometimes located thousands of miles away, use data-driven approaches, which can reinforce traditional power dynamics between international and local actors and hinder efforts for local empowerment. Studies of existing AI tools for humanitarian action reveal that, even when locally generated data is used to train AI models, less than one-third of such models are intended for use by local organizations or crisis-affected populations.[18] Additionally, AI tools are seldom created with the involvement of the local communities that will be impacted by them. A potential solution is to establish locally developed and owned humanitarian AI through participatory AI methodologies, using the collective intelligence of crisis-affected communities as active actors rather than testing beds for emerging AI solutions.[19]

The growing ethical concerns surrounding data collection and technology have led to discussions of "data colonialism," which refers to the exploitation of data and information from marginalized communities by larger and more powerful entities.[20] This can take the form of the appropriation of big data in developing countries by major international powers and big tech companies that claim ownership of and privatize the data produced by their users and citizens. It can also involve using data from indigenous communities without their consent, as well as collecting data from individuals in developing countries or conflict zones and humanitarian emergencies and using it for the benefit of companies or organizations in developed countries. Ethics researchers are pointing out similarities to historical colonialism, in which appropriation of resources took place on a vast scale. Today there is a new grab happening, but it is not land that is being grabbed—it is data.

ETHICS AND DATA RESPONSIBILITY: GENERAL FRAMEWORKS

Only a decade ago, there was almost no discussion about the principles and practice of AI ethics. Since then, technology has often developed faster than our ability to keep up with ethical research.

Beginning with risk cases from real life, thinking about AI ethics has deepened over the years. Yet an AI for peace approach to ethics still needs far more attention, and there is now a great opportunity to learn from and adopt tools and practices already developed from related AI use cases in the humanitarian sector and beyond.

Despite the consensus that AI should be ethical, there is still an active debate on what constitutes "ethical AI." The Alan Turing Institute defines it as a "set of values, principles, and techniques that employ widely accepted standards of right and wrong to guide moral conduct in the development and use of AI technologies."[21] In the past several years, companies, academics, and governments have started issuing principles and guidelines for ethical AI. A few that have received greater visibility in the last several years include the Vatican's "Rome Call for AI Ethics," identifying transparency, inclusion, responsibility, impartiality, reliability, security, and privacy as primary ethical principles[22]; the US Department of Defense's "Ethical Principles for the Use of Artificial Intelligence," with six primary principles: responsible, equitable, traceable, reliable, and governable AI[23]; and the OECD Principles on Artificial Intelligence, promoting AI that is innovative, trustworthy, and respects human rights and democratic values, with a general scope to ensure they can be applied to AI developments around the world.[24]

In 2021, the Recommendation on the Ethics of Artificial Intelligence was adopted by UNESCO's General Conference as the first global standard-setting instrument on the ethics of AI.[25] At the time of writing this chapter, the EU introduced the AI Act, discussed in Chapter 3 on human rights, as the first potential law on AI by a major regulator anywhere, expected to have a broad impact on the use of AI and machine learning for citizens and companies around the world.[26] Some researchers are advocating for a human-rights approach to AI ethics as a more universal and well-defined framework of internationally agreed norms and universal expression of shared values of humanity, which also provides a mechanism for accountability and redress. Laws, however, cannot always keep pace with technological developments, which is why adherence to clear ethical principles is perceived as an additional, sometimes higher standard than formal compliance with laws.

Ethicists consider adherence to AI ethics principles as a pathway to trustworthy AI, another concept dominating the AI ethics discussions. Trust in AI systems is defined as "an attitude that an agent will behave as expected and can be relied upon to reach its goal. Trust breaks down after an error or misunderstanding between the agent and the trusting individual." The EU's Ethics Guidelines for Trustworthy AI define "three components of trustworthy AI that should be met throughout the system's life cycle":

1. It should be lawful, complying with all applicable laws and regulations.
2. It should be ethical, ensuring adherence to ethical principles and values.
3. It should be robust, both from a technical and social perspective, since, even with good intentions, AI systems can cause unintentional harm.[27]

Trustworthy AI aims to "provide the foundation upon which all those affected by AI systems can trust that their design, development, and use are lawful, ethical and robust." Trying to help practitioners to navigate the space of many adopted and proposed principles and guidelines, the OECD created Tools for Trustworthy AI, an interactive database of AI tools, practices, and approaches for implementing trustworthy AI and helping AI practitioners to determine which tool fits their use cases.[28]

A closer look at 84 of these documents containing ethical principles and guidelines for AI shows that they still consist of tools predominantly made in Europe or the United States and are shaped with western-centric ideas, languages, theories, and challenges.[29] Without broader geographic representation, AI ethics will reflect the perspectives of people in only a few regions of the world. Such standards risk the creation of AI systems that perpetuate existing biases, are insensitive to local culture, and repeat the pattern of colonialism. Alternative approaches have been offered as a critique of a prevalent western ethics model and as an attempt to create more global AI ethical thinking, drawing from philosophies such as Buddhism,[30] Ubuntu philosophy,[31] Islamic ethics,[32] or indigenous epistemologies.[33]

AN AI FOR PEACE APPROACH TO ETHICS: RELEVANT RESOURCES

Although existing AI principles and guidelines may have applications for peacebuilding and sustaining peace, none of them explicitly mentions these goals. Some practitioners are advocating for strengthening the essence of ethical AI by adding the terms "sustaining peace" or "peacefulness" to existing principles of fairness, inclusiveness, transparency, privacy, security, and accountability.

There is, however, a concrete demand from members of the AI for peace ecosystem—organizations that are directly applying data science, data-driven, and AI-driven approaches in their specific programs. Peacebuilders still lack sufficient ethical guidelines that have been adopted and are applicable to the new realities of building peace in the age of algorithms. While they can use many of the existing AI ethics tools, the question remains: Are these sufficient to deal with the nuances of peacebuilding, especially in connection to fragile, conflict-affected contexts and vulnerable populations?

One field to which peacebuilders can turn for help is the humanitarian sector. This is because humanitarians working on the issues of refugees, famine, and natural disasters are also often working in active conflict zones with the most vulnerable and marginal populations in the world.[34] Humanitarians are also highly sensitive to the notion of unintended consequences, and they understand that the needs of vulnerable groups require deep expertise rather than one-size-fits-all guidelines, as well as close partnership with local actors and communities.

The UN Office for the Coordination of Humanitarian Affairs (OCHA) Centre for Humanitarian Data focuses on developing guidance, processes, and practices for how OCHA, as the coordinator of humanitarian response, handles humanitarian data. One direct result is the 2021 OCHA Data Responsibility Guidelines to support OCHA's data work.[35] Another important data-responsibility tool is the ICRC's Data Protection Framework, which provides individuals with protection in accordance with international standards.[36] It includes the ICRC Rules on Personal Data Protection along with a supervisory and oversight mechanism. Other relevant resources include the Harvard Humanitarian Initiative's Signal Code,[37] USAID's Considerations for Using Data Responsibly,[38] and IOM's Data Protection Manual,[39] which provide recommendations on how to work responsibly with humanitarian data.

Many of these tools were created as a response to specific risks and real-life cases that demonstrated a need for better AI responsibility. One of the cases investigated by Human Rights Watch in 2021 showed that the UN refugee agency improperly collected and shared personal information from ethnic Rohingya refugees with the Bangladesh government—which then shared it with Myanmar to verify people for possible repatriation, even though this was the country these people fled from in the first place.[40] In crisis-affected and fragile contexts, providing personally identifiable data may be conditionally tied to receiving assistance, raising questions of fairness and consent. Anonymity is also crucial in these settings, where the risk of targeting and reidentification is high. Ethical decision-making would consist of considering the vast power imbalances between international agencies and the people they are protecting, as well as reducing the risk of migrants becoming a test ground for biometric technologies.

One of the widely accepted ethics approaches in conflict settings is "conflict sensitivity," which is a conceptual framework and set of tools that can help different stakeholders navigate the challenges of working in conflict-affected areas. Any organization, company, program, or project operating in a conflict-affected context is very likely to have unintended consequences influencing the situation, which may exacerbate existing conflict dynamics. When organizations operate with algorithms, those consequences can be especially challenging to understand and handle. Conflict-sensitivity approaches can be utilized by any organization as a guideline for tackling complex conflict situations and diminishing the potential negative impact of their activities on violence and conflict. To be conflict-sensitive, an organization should be able to understand the context in which it operates; understand the interaction between its activities and that context; take steps to minimize the negative impacts of its operations; and take steps to maximize the positive effects of its operations for peace.

In this context, the "do no harm" framework is a leading tool. It means that, when applying AI and data, the goal should be to avoid causing any harm or negative consequences and to prioritize the well-being and safety of affected individuals and communities. This approach is based on the idea that the use of AI in these contexts should be carefully considered and controlled in order to ensure that it is used in a way that benefits rather than harms the people it is intended to help. However, almost any data collection and processing in conflict settings comes with some risk of harm (such as in the case of a data breach), so fully embracing the "do no harm" principle would mean not collecting any data. But not collecting any data comes with its own set of possible harms, replacing the risk of misuse of data with the risk of missed use. The challenge is responding to risks without trading off their potential usefulness.

LESSONS LEARNED AND WAY AHEAD

The potential uses of emerging technologies and their risks and consequences are difficult to fully assess. More evidence-based documentation is needed to be able to use the full potential of technological tools while avoiding unintended negative consequences. We opened this chapter with a discussion of the regulatory regime for nuclear weapons. Regulating AI, however, will be much more complex. Nuclear weapons require specific physical materials, making them traceable and controllable through inspections, whereas AI has more widespread applications and mass accessibility. Unlike nuclear weapons, which are highly controlled and limited to a few nations, AI can be developed and deployed across borders by various entities, including private companies and individuals, making comprehensive regulation difficult.

It is critical for organizations that are deploying AI for peace to have both the methodological knowledge and conceptual skills to translate relevant ethical principles into technical terms and implement them in practice. Agreeing on and adopting AI ethics principles is the first step in this process, but the work cannot stop there. Practical methods need to be developed to transfer those principles into practice. And to do both, peacebuilding practitioners need to catch up and stay informed about existing developments and achievements in the AI ethics field and find appropriate ways to transfer those lessons into their own field. The AI for peace ecosystem also needs to be more vocal in bringing the expertise of its own members to the table, specifically integrating the do no harm and conflict sensitivity frameworks into the larger AI ethics field. Ultimately, it will be critical for standard-setting entities on AI ethics to address issues relating to peace, rather than throwing this responsibility back upon individual and often resource-poor organizations.

Recognizing that all projects are different and that processes need to be flexible and adjusted to the cultural context in which the project is designed and implemented are both important. However, minimum standards, principles, and values, such as those set by the UNESCO AI ethics work, should be adopted and considered universal. These robust ethics risk assessments are needed to ensure AI is used responsibly in response to conflict or for sustaining peace work.

There is a key challenge, however. Peacebuilding work is often implemented at a moment of crisis, making the use of ethical principles—which may require longer time horizons to assess impact—difficult. In the context of a crisis, conflict, and fragility, there may be a trade-off between a cautious approach and the need to deploy an AI project quickly. When the situation is fragile and changing at unprecedented speed, and when early action usually means saving lives but often comes with additional risks, there may also be a need to develop an "ethics in crisis," which does not yet exist. This does not mean that ethical norms and processes should be skipped or neglected, but rather emphasizes the need to design appropriate processes for embedding ethics with urgency in these contexts.[41] This is an ethics to be invented, and along with the issues above, it will be essential to realizing the promise of AI for peace.

NOTES

1 "Atoms for Peace Speech – Address by Mr. Dwight D. Eisenhower, President of the United States of America, to the 470th Plenary Meeting of the United Nations General Assembly," *International Atomic Energy Agency;* accessed November 15, 2022, https://www.iaea.org/about/history/atoms-for-peace-speech.

2 "Facial Recognition Tool Led to Mistaken Arrest, Lawyer Says," *NBC News,* January 4, 2023, https://www.nbcnews.com/tech/security/facial-recognition-tool-led-mistaken-arrest-lawyer-says-rcna64270.

3 International Committee of the Red Cross, "Artificial Intelligence and Machine Learning in Armed Conflict: A Human-Centred Approach," June 6, 2019, https://www.icrc.org/en/document/artificial-intelligence-and-machine-learning-armed-conflict-human-centred-approach.

4 Ruairi Nolan, "Ethics in Peacebuilding." *Peace Insight,* April 21, 2010, https://www.peaceinsight.org/en/articles/ethics-in-peacebuilding/?location=&theme=.

5 Slim, Hugo. *Humanitarian Ethics: A Guide to the Morality of Aid in War and Disaster.* London: Hurst & Company, 2015. https://doc-center.ocg.msf.org/index.php?lvl=notice_display&id=6457.

6 "Handbook on Data Protection in Humanitarian Action," *International Committee of the Red Cross,* May 28, 2020, https://www.icrc.org/en/data-protection-humanitarian-action-handbook.

7 Nathaniel Raymond, Laura Walker McDonald, and Rahul Chandran, "Opinion: The WFP and Palantir Controversy Should Be a Wake-up Call for Humanitarian Community," Devex, February 14, 2019. https://www.devex.com/news/opinion-the-wfp-and-palantir-controversy-should-be-a-wake-up-call-for-humanitarian-community-94307.

8 Faine Greenwood, "The Crucial Need to Secure the Location Data of Vulnerable Populations," *Brookings*, last modified December 17, 2021, https://www.brookings.edu/techstream/the-crucial-need-to-secure-the-location-data-of-vulnerable-populations/.

9 Raphael Satter, "Exclusive: Google Locks Afghan Government Accounts as Taliban Seek Emails -Source." *Reuters*, September 4, 2021, https://www.reuters.com/world/asia-pacific/exclusive-google-locks-afghan-government-accounts-taliban-seek-emails-source-2021-09-03/.

10 Elizabeth Culliford, "Google Temporarily Disables Google Maps Live Traffic Data in Ukraine," *Reuters*, February 28, 2022, https://www.reuters.com/technology/google-temporarily-disables-google-maps-live-traffic-data-ukraine-2022-02-28/.

11 Amy Kraft, "Microsoft Shuts down AI Chatbot, Tay, after It Turned into a Nazi." *CBS News*, March 25, 2016. https://www.cbsnews.com/news/microsoft-shuts-down-ai-chatbot-after-it-turned-into-racist-nazi/.

12 Mekhail Mustak, Joni Salminen, Matti Mäntymäki, Arafat Rahman, and Yogesh K. Dwivedi, "Deepfakes: Deceptions, Mitigations, and Opportunities," *Journal of Business Research* 154 (January, 2023), accessed July 1, 2023, https://doi.org/10.1016/j.jbusres.2022.113368.

13 Maxine Danso, "Dated, Doctored and False: The Facts about Viral Video Purporting Akufo-Addo Was Caught Receiving $40,000 Bribe as President," *Dubawa Ghana*, December 4, 2020, https://ghana.dubawa.org/dated-doctored-and-false-the-facts-about-the-viral-video-purporting-akufo-addo-was-caught-receiving-a-40000-bribe-as-president/.

14 Jackson Cote, "Deepfakes and Fake News Pose a Growing Threat to Democracy, Experts Warn," Northeastern Global News, April 1, 2022, https://news.northeastern.edu/2022/04/01/deepfakes-fake-news-threat-democracy/.

15 "Cyber-Attack on ICRC: What We Know." *ICRC*, January 21, 2022, accessed December 16, 2022, https://www.icrc.org/en/document/cyber-attack-icrc-what-we-know.

16 Fabio Urbina, Filippa Lentzos, Cédric Invernizzi, and Sean Ekins, "Dual Use of Artificial-Intelligence-Powered Drug Discovery." *Nature Machine Intelligence* 4, (March 2022): 189–191, https://doi.org/10.1038/s42256-022-00465-9.

17 Sarah W. Spencer, "Humanitarian AI - The Hype, the Hope and the Future," *Humanitarian Practice Network*, Number 85. (November 2021), https://odihpn.org/wp-content/uploads/2021/11/HPN-Network-Paper_AI_web_181121.pdf.

18 Aleks, Berditchevskaiia, Eirini Malliaraki, Kathy Peach, Oil Whittington, Issy Gill, "Collective Crisis Intelligence for Frontline Humanitarian Response," *Nesta*, September 15, 2021, https://www.nesta.org.uk/report/collective-crisis-intelligence-frontline-humanitarian-response/.

19 "Participatory AI for Humanitarian Innovation: A Briefing Paper," *Nesta*, Accessed July 1, 2023. https://www.nesta.org.uk/report/participatory-ai-humanitarian-innovation-briefing-paper/.

20 Nanjala Nyabola and Antonia Baskakov, "Data Colonialism, Digital Rights, and the Role of Civil Society - an Interview with Nanjala Nyabola and Antonia Baskakov," BMZ Digital.Global, November 30, 2022, https://www.bmz-digital.global/en/datacolonialism-double-interview/.

21 See The Alan Turing Institute website at https://www.turing.ac.uk/

22 "Rome Call for AI Ethics: A Global University Summit," *Tech Ethics Lab*, Accessed July 1, 2023. https://techethicslab.nd.edu/news-and-events/rome-call-for-ai-ethics-a-global-university-summit/.

23 "DOD Adopts Ethical Principles for Artificial Intelligence," *U.S. Department of Defense*, February 24, 2020, https://www.defense.gov/News/Releases/Release/Article/2091996/dod-adopts-ethical-principles-for-artificial-intelligence/.

24 "The OECD Artificial Intelligence (AI) Principles," OECD, 2019, https://oecd.ai/en/ai-principles.

25 "Elaboration of a Recommendation on the Ethics of Artificial Intelligence," UNESCO, February 27, 2020, https://en.unesco.org/artificial-intelligence/ethics.

26 See the EU AI Act website at https://artificialintelligenceact.eu/.

27 "Ethics Guidelines for Trustworthy AI | Shaping Europe's Digital Future," European Commission, April 8, 2019, https://digital-strategy.ec.europa.eu/en/library/ethics-guidelines-trustworthy-ai.

28 "What Are the Tools for Implementing Trustworthy AI? A Comparative Framework and Database," OECD.AI, May 25, 2021, https://oecd.ai/en/wonk/tools-for-trustworthy-ai.

29 Anna Jobin, Marcello Ienca, and Effy Vayena, "The Global Landscape of AI Ethics Guidelines," *Nature Machine Intelligence* 1 (2019): 389–99, https://doi.org/10.1038/s42256-019-0088-2.

30 Soraj Hongladarom, "What Buddhism Can Do for AI Ethics," *MIT Technology Review*, January 6, 2021, https://www.technologyreview.com/2021/01/06/1015779/what-buddhism-can-do-ai-ethics/.

31 Sabelo Mhlambi, "From Rationality to Relationality: Ubuntu as an Ethical and Human Rights Framework for Artificial Intelligence Governance." *Carr Center Discussion Paper Series*, no. 2020-009, July 8, 2020, https://carrcenter.hks.harvard.edu/publications/rationality-relationality-ubuntu-ethical-and-human-rights-framework-artificial.

32 Amana Raquib, *Islamic Ethics of Technology: An Objectives' (Maqasid) Approach* (Kuala Lumpur, The Other Press, 2015).

33 Jason Edward Lewis, Angie Abdilla, Noelani Arista, Kaipulaumakaniolono Baker, Scott Benesiinaabandan, Michelle Brown, Melanie Cheung, et al, "Indigenous Protocol and Artificial Intelligence Position Paper," April 15, 2020, https://spectrum.library.concordia.ca/id/eprint/986506/.

34 Kate Dodgson, Dr. Prithvi Hirani, Rob Trigwell and Gretchen Bueermann, "A Framework for the ethical use of Advanced Data Science Methods in Humanitarian Field," *Data Science Ethics Group*, January 4, 2020, https://www.hum-dseg.org/sites/g/files/tmzbdl1476/files/2020-10/Framework%20for%20the%20ethical%20use.pdf.

35 "OCHA Data Responsibility Guidelines," *The Centre for Humanitarian Data*, accessed December 7, 2022, https://centre.humdata.org/data-responsibility/.

36 "The ICRC Data Protection Framework," *ICRC*, June 2, 2020, https://www.icrc.org/en/document/icrc-data-protection-framework.

37 Faine Greenwood, Caitlin Howarth, Danielle Escudero Poole, Nathaniel A. Raymond, and Daniel P. Scarnecchia, "The Signal Code: A Human Rights Approach to Information during Crisis," *Harvard Humanitarian Initiative*, January 2017, https://hhi.harvard.edu/publications/signal-code-human-rights-approach-information-during-crisis.

38 "Considerations for Using Data Responsibly at USAID," *USAID*, May 1, 2022. https://www.usaid.gov/responsibledata.

39 "IOM Data Protection Manual," *International Organization for Migration*, October 7, 2015, accessed July 1, 2023. https://www.iom.int/news/iom-publishes-data-protection-manual.

40 "UN Shared Rohingya Data Without Informed Consent," *Human Rights Watch*, June 15, 2021. https://www.hrw.org/news/2021/06/15/un-shared-rohingya-data-without-informed-consent.

41 Asaf Tzachor, Jess Whittlestone, Lalitha Sundaram, and Seán Ó hÉigeartaigh, "Artificial Intelligence in a Crisis Needs Ethics with Urgency," *Nature Machine Intelligence* 2 (2020): 365–366, https://doi.org/10.1038/s42256-020-0195-0.

Printed in the United States
by Baker & Taylor Publisher Services